AMERICAN IMPERIALISM
Viewpoints of United States
Foreign Policy, 1898-1941

*Reproduced with the cooperation of the
Hoover Institution of War, Revolution and Peace,
Stanford University, Stanford, California*

THE AMERICANS IN SANTO DOMINGO

Melvin M. Knight

ARNO PRESS & THE NEW YORK TIMES
New York ★ 1970

Collection Created and Selected
by
CHARLES GREGG OF GREGG PRESS

Reprinted from a copy in The Hoover Institution Library

Library of Congress Catalog Card Number: 75-111722
ISBN 0-405-02032-5

ISBN for complete set: 0-405-02000-7

Reprint Edition 1970 by Arno Press Inc.
Manufactured in the United States of America

AMERICAN IMPERIALISM

*American Fund for Public Service Studies
in American Investments Abroad*

*Edited, with Introduction,
By* HARRY ELMER BARNES

*Studies in
American Imperialism*

The Americans in Santo Domingo

By MELVIN M. KNIGHT

NEW YORK
VANGUARD PRESS

Copyright, 1928, by
VANGUARD PRESS, INC.

VANGUARD PRINTINGS
First—February, 1928

PRINTED IN THE UNITED STATES OF AMERICA

EDITOR'S INTRODUCTION

WHAT is usually known as modern economic imperialism is one of the most characteristic and important historical developments of contemporary times. It is not only a leading phase of modern commerce and investment, but has also profoundly affected other aspects of our life. In the field of politics it has involved both the development of a foreign policy conditioned by overseas ambitions and colonial dominion, and the reaction of this type of foreign policy upon the domestic political institutions of those states which have participated to any extensive degree in imperialistic ventures. As L. T. Hobhouse long ago made clear, no country can devote a part of its energy and resources to the acquisition and domination of lands and peoples overseas and still hope to keep its domestic politics free from the responsibilities and handicaps imposed by overseas dominion. In the field of social institutions far-reaching modifications have been produced both at home and abroad through the contact of widely different cultures. Likewise, culture and intellectual life have been deeply influenced by that interaction of divergent cultures upon each other which has been produced through the contacts promoted by modern imperialism. Therefore, it may be contended with full assurance of accuracy and moderation that one who fails to acquaint himself with the nature and achievements of contemporary imperialism will have ignored one of the most significant phases of contemporary civilization. Inattention to contemporary imperialistic activity not only marks one out as deplorably ignorant of vital issues, but also renders one incapable of coping intelligently with many of the more pressing and baffling problems of present-day politics and international relations. It represents a type of ignorance which is not only humiliating but positively dangerous. Almost worse than blank ignorance, however, is that Pollyanna attitude of benign trust and cosmic complacency which is born of acquaintance with the issues of modern imperialism through the medium of the conventional journals or party channels that assures us of the complete benevolence of investors and of the deaf ear which foreign offices and state departments invariably turn to all appeals to put the force of an imperialistic nation behind the requests of interested investors and merchants.

It is obvious that the particular manifestation of contemporary imperialism most interesting and relevant to Americans is the expansion of American capital and colonial power beyond the ancient boundaries of the United States. It has often been stated by patriotic orators that the United States is the one state which has resolutely stood aloof from the imperialistic orgy of the last half century. The truth would seem to be rather that we were conceived in imperialism and dedicated to the principle of expansion. Founded as a phase of the first great period of imperialism and colonialism, we have always been an imperialistic country from the standpoint of the development of control over new areas and the subjugation of lower peoples. The history of our country has been in one sense the record of imperialistic efforts and successes. The history of the United States from 1607 to 1890 is the chronicle of a continually expanding frontier, during which process we brought the original Indian population under our control and conquered most of a great continent. This phase ended about 1890, at the very time when we had just passed through the most important stages of the Industrial Revolution, had for the first time acquired a considerable volume of excess capital and had developed a greater need for markets overseas. In other words, we appeared to need to expand beyond our boundaries at the exact moment when we had the resources to do so and were under the control of a political party that was to a peculiar degree dominated by American industry and finance.

It was natural that we should first turn to Latin America, justifying our action in official rhetoric on the ground of advancing the cause of human justice, but not failing in the process to improve the facilities for investment and the acquisition of the valuable natural resources of the lands occupied. Our intervention in Cuba was not in any sense a novel or cataclysmic affair. We had aided the movements for Cuban independence from Spain and had considered intervention at various times for more than half a century before 1898. At that time things shaped up in such a way that we took the final step. From Cuba we extended our economic penetration and political pressure into other parts of Latin America: Mexico, Haiti, Santo Domingo, Nicaragua, Honduras, Panama and the Virgin Islands. During the same period we turned to the Pacific and entered the Hawaiian Islands, the Philippines and China. With the outbreak of the World War came our remarkable investments in Allied bonds and the subsequent European loans which have made us the most powerful factor in European finance. With the discovery of rich petroleum resources in Asia Minor and Mesopotamia, we have interested ourselves in the Near East. There is apparently no discernible limit to the nature or extent of our future investments in overseas areas.

Much heat and dogmatism have been expended in the efforts to define and describe contemporary imperialism. Some regard it chiefly as an economic process; others as extension of political domination. To some it appears a benevolent civilizing process; to others it seems the most brutal and heartless manifestation of modern capitalism and the spirit of acquisitiveness. To the writer it appears that it is best to abandon for the time being any of the old single-track dogmas concerning imperialism and to make a careful study of the actual facts, in order that we may find out just what contemporary imperialism really amounts to. In so doing we may find that some of our older dogmas are completely discredited, while other assumptions may be verified and extended. We have conventionally assumed that the imperialistic process is essentially the following:

> 1. Merchants and bankers recognize the opportunities for pecuniary gain in certain relatively backward political and economic areas.
> 2. Their penetration is followed by appeals to the foreign offices of their respective states.
> 3. These requests lead immediately to military intervention and the political administration of such areas.

Such a sequence, while not uncommon, is by no means inevitable. In many cases there is no intervention at all because the bankers and merchants feel that they can carry on their activities to better effect without the embarrassment of political friction. Yet we have to be on our guard against assuming that economic penetration without political protection is invariably less harmful or less menacing to the freedom of backward states than overt political domination. It is more subtle and may be more dangerous. Hence, what is most needed is a series of concrete studies of imperialism in action. This does not imply that we shall emerge as eulogists of imperialism. We may end by formulating a more vigorous indictment of imperialism than that conventionally offered by socialistically inclined writers or we may discover that in some respects the imperialistic process is mitigated by the achievements. What we need is the facts before we can construct either a convincing condemnation or a telling defense of imperialism. After all, as we have now come to agree in the social sciences, what a thing does is much more important than what it is; indeed, the best notion of what a thing is can be obtained from a thorough knowledge of what it does. A knowledge of the processes of imperialism is far more valuable than the scholastic exercise of formulating a comprehensive definition.

Further, we need to relinquish the somewhat simple-minded hypothesis of the conscious, overt and undeviating diabolism of contemporary imperialism. There is no doubt that, as society is organized today, we have certain definite economic needs which can only be met by obtaining markets overseas and by securing raw materials from foreign areas. We have accumulated a large surplus of capital for investment which will inevitably seek an outlet beyond our national boundaries. We have to consider frankly such economic realities. We are likely to be faced for a long time with the problem of the contact of higher and lower cultures, of so-called superior and inferior economic systems. As long as the prevailing types of political and economic organization continue, we shall have to face this issue of economic penetration and political dominion. If we desire to modify or eliminate this situation, we shall have to operate, in part at least indirectly, in the way of changing the nature or the economic, political and social organization of humanity. Yet we need not accept the naïve belief that with the progress of socialism imperialism will at once disappear. If we could have a world-wide socialistic revolution which successfully carried into immediate execution the transition from an acquisitive economy based upon private profit to one founded on the objective of production for social service, then indeed imperialism might disappear rapidly. It is probable, however, that if socialism triumphs, it will be a gradual process in which the socialistic states will have to face hostile and greedy capitalistic polities. Under these conditions the socialistic commonwealths can scarcely surrender meekly to their capitalistic rivals the indispensable raw materials and markets essential to the happiness and prosperity of their citizens. Imperialism would not immediately disappear with socialism, but would constitute one of those knotty problems with which socialism would have to deal in order to remain consistent with its theoretical pretensions. One thing is certain, namely, that socialist and capitalist alike, if honest and intelligent, must unite in desiring the facts in the premises, and that is what this series of studies in modern imperialism has been designed to produce.

The American Fund for Public Service is engaged in the process of employing a considerable sum of money for the purpose of advancing in divers ways the cause of human enlightenment and social justice. It was conceived, and probably justly, that one way in which this goal could be attained would be the appropriation of an adequate fund to allow the prosecution of studies into American expansion and investment. The organization rendered substantial aid in the process of compiling and publishing the notable books by Nearing and Freeman on *Dollar Diplomacy* and by Mr. Dunn on *American Foreign Investments*. It was further decided to carry out several intensive investigations of typical examples of American imperialism under the general direction of the present writer. Cuba, Santo Domingo and Bolivia were first selected for this purpose. Cuba is an example of a theoretically independent state which has become in fact an economic protectorate and also occupies a peculiar political status owing to the Platt Amendment and the consequent ability of the United States to protect economic investment by periodic political intervention. Santo Domingo is a representative sample of forceful intervention to protect American investors. Bolivia presents a case where the penetration has thus far been purely economic, and in which the engagements of the government of the state involved have been made primarily with the private bankers who have floated the requested loans.

For the execution of these studies into American Investments Abroad three highly competent investigators were engaged. Dr. Melvin M. Knight, a trained historian and economist, a professional student of contemporary economic history, and a specialist in the subject of colonial government was selected to study Santo Domingo. Dr. Leland H. Jenks, likewise trained equally in history and economics, and a specialist who has demonstrated his competence in this field by producing the foremost work on the migration of British capital overseas, has been entrusted with the task of dealing with the Cuban situation. Margaret Alexander Marsh, long well known for her interest in international affairs, for a considerable period executive secretary of the American Association for International Conciliation, and a specialist for the Federal Council of Churches on American investments in Mexico, was chosen to investigate the situation in Bolivia.

It is hoped that public interest in the enterprise will be sufficient to warrant a continuance of these studies until they have covered the chief areas of American investment and intervention in Latin America.

It remains now only to speak briefly of Dr. Knight's work. To the writer of this introduction it appears that he has achieved a conspicuous success in presenting the essentials in the story of the contact of the United States with Santo Domingo with clarity and freedom from animus. He has manifestly been motivated solely by the effort to get at the truth and to present it in an effective manner. To do so he has mastered all the cogent facts and set them forth in an engaging manner, lightened by humor and illumined by such sagacious generalizations as the basic facts permit. It is difficult to see how either a capitalist or a socialist, if interested in mastering realities, could well challenge Dr. Knight's acquaintance with the facts or condemn the spirit in which he has organized and presented these facts. No candid American citizen can read his account and fail to have a more intelligent and chastened view of his country's participation in the economic penetration of the lands beyond our continental borders.

Northampton, Mass., HARRY ELMER BARNES.
January, 1928.

PREFACE

In the concluding chapter of this brief study, an attempt is made to give some of the reasons why the general public knows so little about American business in countries like Santo Domingo. A succinct statement may be of some value at the outset.

To begin with, very few people out of a thousand have any clear idea of the technique of public finance, or of private business involving a heavy initial investment which is recovered only after a period of years, even in the United States. Everyone cannot be a financial expert, any more than he can be a doctor or a civil engineer, in addition to his regular occupation. The planning of sinking fund payments, the calculation of overhead costs and the estimation of the probable market value of securities from the term they run, the yield and the degree of safety offered are operations which will continue to be carried on by the specially trained and experienced. Even the most skillful financiers sometimes have issues left on their hands. This is especially true of foreign bonds.

The difficulty of grasping the conditions under which business is carried on in countries whose climates, soils and peoples are unfamiliar, is much greater. Money is loaned to governments or invested in private enterprises in regions like Santo Domingo because the returns promised are larger. Higher interest rates prevail in our Southern and Western states than in New York, and still higher ones in Santo Domingo, Haiti or Nicaragua. One of the two main elements back of these differences is the fear which lenders have of unfamiliar conditions. The other is the actual risk involved, and is thus related to the first. When an American investor hires out his capital in Santo Domingo, we might say he is betting that the unavoidable risk is less than the money market indicates—in other words, that the higher returns promised more than cover it.

Here is where the trouble begins. The banker, merchant or sugar planter who operates where the standard return is 10 or 12 percent can borrow the capital at about half that rate in the United States if only he can convince the smaller lenders that he is really assuming the extra risk. Similarly, a New York bank can get $5\frac{1}{2}$ percent or more on conservative loans to the Dominican Government, though the same investors will buy American Government bonds yielding $4\frac{1}{2}$ percent, or less. Having placed capital in the public bonds of Santo Domingo, or in private ventures there, at these higher rates, the business man tries to hedge it about with the same guarantees which prevail in the United States.

Intervention may occur later for either one of two economic reasons, or a combination of them. The political and military factors are too complicated to discuss in a preface, and must be left over for treatment in the chapters which follow. If the Dominican Government fails to pay the interest, or if the principal seems in danger, the big lenders are practically certain to ask their government (or governments) to exact compliance with "the principles recognized by all civilized nations." Likewise, if the 10 percent or the principal due on private loans is in jeopardy, the investors may feel that their Government should bring pressure upon that of

Santo Domingo to enforce the same set of "recognized principles." These are nothing more or less than the conventions of modern business, as conducted in industrialized countries. One of them is that capital placed legally and in good faith where it is tied up for a period of years shall be more or less safe from confiscation. In practice, interventions take place much more frequently because of government obligations than over private loans, concessions or other business.

Most cases, including that of Santo Domingo, are more complicated than this. A number of the Dominican public loans have been practically guaranteed, and collections supervised, by the United States Government. The advantage for the borrowing country is that the added security makes a lower interest rate possible. Under these circumstances, the banking business involved is extremely profitable for someone. The bank designated as official depositary gets the use of considerable sums at American rates and is able to put out much of this money at Dominican private rates, which are about twice as high. If it is a New York bank, as it has been since 1917, it is certain to use this official nucleus to place still further amounts, obtainable at New York rates but yielding the much higher Dominican returns.

At this point we get to the heart of the matter. Land and labor are absurdly cheap in Santo Domingo. A common laborer gets about 60 cents a day, and good sugar land can be had at a fraction of the price demanded in Louisiana, Cuba or Porto Rico. Americans prefer to loan money to American planters, or better still to form big sugar corporations whose directorates interlock with that of the lending bank. These companies exploit the cheap Dominican land, largely with imported Haitian and other outside black West Indian labor—the worst paid in the Western Hemisphere. This tends to keep wages down, and to put more and more of the surface of the country under foreign ownership. Moreover, the companies have stores which sell to their own employees—imported Haitians at the bottom and imported Americans at the top. Thus mercantile enterprise, as well as agriculture, falls partially into foreign hands. The economic cancer is the alien control of huge tracts of the best land. If this sore could be removed by an operation, another might break out. That is a question which can be answered only when it is really posed.

American business keeps many things secret from its own government. This is in part to guard them from competitors. The evasion of taxes is also to be considered as a factor. Without any political schemes at all, our highly organized Bureau of Foreign and Domestic Commerce would inevitably promote many things of vast political consequence simply because of its blindness to other matters than the furthering of private business. Some abuses which arise from this situation are harder to forestall than an organized plot, with the United States Government as a party, would be. Another disconcerting fact which is not generally faced is that a perfectly legal and well intentioned American enterprise may do far more damage to a weak country in the long run than a fraudulent promotion scheme. The latter is less likely to injure natives than the incautious Americans who buy the stock.

The material for this study was gathered mainly in Santo Domingo, Washington and New York. I also visited Haiti and Porto Rico, and was already more or less familiar with Cuba and Jamaica. It seemed wise to establish some comparisons, especially with Haiti, where so much of the labor comes from and where American military supervision is still operating. The expense has been borne by the American Fund for Public Service. An advisory committee of scholars in history and international law, practising attorneys and other specially qualified people gave valuable advice, but never interfered in any way with the work. The author is solely responsible for any views expressed. Judge Otto Schoenrich, whose excellent general work, *Santo Domingo, a Country with a Future,* is well known, made many helpful suggestions at the outset, and was extremely generous about loans of material. Barnard College, Columbia University, with which the writer was connected at the time as Assistant Professor of History, kindly granted a year's leave of absence.

The rather bulky two-volume typewritten report submitted in the fall of 1926 was so detailed, and in places so technical, that the Committee felt it would be more serviceable if shortened and simplified for publication in book form. Seeing the reasonableness of this suggestion, I have done my best under rather difficult conditions. Other duties have intervened, and North Africa is somewhat isolated from either Santo Domingo or Washington. The present MS. represents about a fourth of the material in the report. I have tried to pick the fourth of most use to the probable readers of a book on this subject. A study of this kind, compiled largely from a mass of official publications and notes taken on the ground, could not in any case give more than a small fraction of the actual documents. Even the most important would quickly run into volumes. I have marked the appendices of the original report for omission, as the general reader will not need them, and the special student would want much more. The notes on sources should enable the latter to find the original material without too much trouble.

It is perhaps needless to remark that some errors must have been committed in the course of noting, translating, condensing, copying and editing such a mass of material. Reviewers usually catch the most glaring of these. Others who may find them will do the author a favor if they will write him, in care of the publishers, so that corrections can be made. Especially do the Spanish accents have a way of slipping out, in the hands of American and French typists. More conscious of the sum total of its shortcoming than anybody else could be, I offer the study for publication in this form merely in the hope that it may be useful, and throw some light on one specific case in a very difficult group of problems.

Algiers, *April, 1927.* M. M. KNIGHT.

CONTENTS

Chapter		Page
	EDITOR'S INTRODUCTION	v
	PREFACE	xiii
I.	INHERITING THE SPANISH MAIN	1
II.	PRESIDENT GRANT—AND THE AMERICAN WEST INDIA COMPANY	6
III.	THE SAN DOMINGO IMPROVEMENT COMPANY	14
IV.	PRESIDENT ROOSEVELT'S TWO RECEIVERSHIPS	26
V.	THE FAILURE OF THE ROOSEVELT POLICY	40
VI.	THE RULE OF DESERVING DEMOCRATS	53
VII.	FROM THREATS TO FORCE	67
VIII.	SETTING UP A MILITARY DICTATORSHIP	86
IX.	THE REORGANIZATION OF SANTO DOMINGO, 1916-1922	97
X.	MILITARY JUSTICE FOR CIVILIANS	108
XI.	GETTING RID OF THE MARINES	119
XII.	SUGAR—A CASE OF INDUSTRIAL FEUDALISM	129
XIII.	ECONOMIC PENETRATION	144
XIV.	IS THERE A "YANKEE PERIL?"	161
	REFERENCE NOTES BY CHAPTERS	177

THE AMERICANS IN SANTO DOMINGO

CHAPTER I

INHERITING THE SPANISH MAIN

In spite of the process of continuous expansion, which the survey of the history of the United States discloses, there can be no doubt that there exists among the American people a belief that they are characterized above all things by freedom from territorial ambitions and a peculiarly peace-loving disposition.—JOHN BASSETT MOORE.

THE American business men in Santo Domingo who tried a little too hard to get President Grant to annex the country soon after our Civil War were not the authors of all the problems they rudely attempted to solve. It was not they who had killed off the original population which Columbus had found so friendly, and so exceptionally happy, when the first permanent European colony in the New World was founded. Neither were they responsible for the presence of people whose ancestors had been brought from Africa against their will, to bear the intruding white man's burdens for him.

Before the thirteen American colonies had become a nation, European imperial policies and private greed had indelibly written a great deal of Caribbean history.

Spaniards, Englishmen, Dutchmen, Frenchmen and international freebooters had fought and plundered each other for centuries. They had marked out the best routes and the key positions. The eastern gateways to Panama and the Gulf of Mexico are in the West Indies. One of the main causes of the American Revolution had arisen from the traffic in black men, and the sugar and molasses which their toil contributed to make New England rum so justly famous.

Three main groups of problems have stood out in American public policies and private enterprises in the Caribbean islands from the beginning. First, the situation of this crescent known as the Greater and Lesser Antilles on the highways of empire has led to the application of a Monroe Doctrine, expanded into a policy of intervention. Second, the value of the islands in their own right has given rise to economic penetration. Third, the color line in the United States has confused everything else we have tried to do because we have not been able to project it abroad or find any solution for it at home.

From the time when Haiti and Santo Domingo freed themselves from their European masters up to our Civil War, we could have no normal relations with black or mulatto republics hardly more than a day's journey from our Southern States, where African slavery prevailed. Neither Haiti nor Santo Domingo was recognized until secession withdrew the Southern votes from our Congress. These two little states—separated by the Dominican war for independence in 1844—were treated practically as footballs by the parties, pro and con, to the domestic issue of slavery in the United States. The Panama Congress of American Republics, held in 1826, was torn by the question of Haitian participation and

accomplished almost nothing. Under the famous "Gag
Rule" of 1836, which tabled all petitions for Abolition,
the Abolitionists submitted memorials on Haitian recognition instead, amid Southern cries of "treason" and
"nefarious designs." A Southern Senator asserted that
the campaign was not even "for the paltry commerce
of a horde of barbarians," and he told the exact truth.
A pro-slavery move to recognize Santo Domingo separately, on the ground that her population was largely
white, was killed by Charles Sumner and a group of
Northern journalists, mainly by the submission of proof
that most of the public men of that republic had colored
ancestry.[1]

The Monroe Doctrine of 1823 was purely defensive
in its original setting. It was drawn up in the face of a
threatened intervention by the Quadruple Alliance (of
the four monarchs of Russia, Austria, Prussia and
France) to restore Spain's authority in her revolted
American colonies. George Canning, then British Foreign Secretary, effectively supported American opposition; but the United States Government went much
farther. Besides recognizinig the new Latin-American
Governments, which Canning refused to do, Monroe
laid down the famous general principles: (1) That these
continents were closed to future European colonization;
(2) That we could not tolerate European intervention,
which we must consider a menace to our peace and
safety. This policy, balanced by a certain aloofness on
our part from purely European disputes, was much older
than 1823, but Monroe's is the classic statement of it.
The substance can be found in the writings of Washington and Jefferson.

How Manifest Destiny—which at its worst has been
a mixture of Pan-Americanism and *Gott Mit Uns*—

came to be read into Monroe's arguments for self-defense is largely the history of a series of logical afterthoughts. Diplomats, when they use the jargon of the profession, are prone to say less than they hope they mean, but to express themselves loosely enough to make room for future developments. Jumping clear down to the Venezuela dispute with Great Britain in 1895 in order to make the accumulation of meaning clear, we find Secretary of State Olney making the belligerent declaration that: "To-day, the United States is practically sovereign on this continent, and its fiat is law upon the subjects to which it confines its interposition." In the end, we justified interventions of our own on the ground that we could not properly prevent European ones without removing any just grievances which seemed to call for them.

How the balance of power in the Caribbean has regulated the effectiveness of the Monroe Doctrine may be illustrated by a glance at our relations with Santo Domingo after 1850. In 1851, we entered into the curious Tri-Partite Agreement with France and Great Britain for the protection of the Dominican Republic against the Empire of Haiti.[2] This turned out to be a farce. Great Britain was keeping France out by threats of occupying Haiti herself. The United States wanted Samana Bay, in eastern Santo Domingo, for a naval base, but did not dare to take it because of British and French opposition. Captain (later General) George B. McClellan made a thorough survey of the harbor of Samana in 1854, in connection with a new deal for its acquisition by the United States.[3] This was cleverly blocked by the British and French, who aroused the fears of the Dominicans on the question of American negro slavery. During the same year appeared the famous

Ostend Manifesto, which made Spain apprehensive of our Cuban plans and added one more power to the restraining circle.

Haiti was recognized by the United States during the Civil War. Santo Domingo handed herself back to Spain at the opening of that struggle, for fear that worse might happen. This was an unhappy arrangement. A revolution soon broke out, and the Spaniards were finally ejected just at the close of the War of Secession in the United States. The way was open for the imperial schemes of Seward and Grant.

CHAPTER II

PRESIDENT GRANT—AND THE AMERICAN WEST INDIA COMPANY

> "I weep for you," the walrus said;
> "I deeply sympathize";
> With sobs and tears, he sorted out
> Those of the largest size,
> Holding his pocket handkerchief
> Before his streaming eyes.
>
> LEWIS CARROLL

GENERAL WILLIAM L. CAZNEAU founded the American West India Company in 1862, shortly after he had ceased to represent the American Government in Santo Domingo. This man was nominally a Texan, though he had been born in Massachusetts of French Roman Catholic ancestry. He had learned Spanish and the art of armed infiltration during years of adventuring on the Mexican border. His long and troubled connection with Dominican affairs had begun in 1854, when he accompanied McClellan as an envoy of the United States Government. During the Civil War he was denounced for Southern sympathies and treasonable utterances against President Lincoln. This was the main reason assigned for the failure of his candidacy for the proposed post of American Minister a little later. The State Department suddenly decided not to have a Minister just yet, and afterward made it a practice to warn its Commercial

THE AMERICAN WEST INDIA COMPANY 7

Agents and other representatives against Cazneau, who was suspected of being shifty, if not dishonest.

Associated with Cazneau in the American West India Company, according to its prospectuses,[1] were the following: Hiram Ketchum, of 29 William Street, New York City, President; George F. Dunning, described as "Superintendent, U. S. Assay Office," Treasurer; Joseph W. Fabens, No. 6 Pine Street, New York City, Secretary; and Richard B. Kimball, 49 Wall Street, New York City. Cazneau was mentioned in this comparatively late prospectus of 1865 as "late U. S. Special Envoy." Of the five trustees, three gave addresses in the heart of New York's financial district, and the other two paraded their connections, or former connections, with the United States Government.

This scheme was sold to the Government in Santo Domingo as a colonizing enterprise on the early Texas model, which would place armed Americans with property interests at stake between the more settled part of Santo Domingo and the Haitian frontier. Its history came out in the Hatch Investigation of 1870.[2] The million dollar capital was represented by a real estate concession which was later canceled for non-fulfillment of terms, and a few thousands of dollars invested in actual promotion. One group of deluded settlers was chased out by the revolution against Spain. The remnant of the next which did not die of fever was shipped back home by the American Commercial Agent. Cazneau's concession hunting was a standing joke in Santo Domingo, but his influence was tragic. Under the Grant Administration, he had a way of carelessly exhibiting correspondence from Washington, written on Executive Mansion letterheads, and succeeded in completely undermining the influence of the Commercial

8   THE AMERICANS IN SANTO DOMINGO

Agents who officially represented the State Department.

Fabens, described at the time as a speculator and promoter without any regular business, had a career in Santo Domingo second in interest only to that of Cazneau. He stated before the Hatch Investigating Committee that he had no financial interest in Cazneau's land project after it was reorganized as the San Domingo Cotton Company in 1866. He admitted, however, that Cazneau was a party to his own still broader scheme for a geological survey of all the public lands of Santo Domingo. For this service, the group was to get one-fifth of the land, to be claimed as the survey went on. Fabens appeared as the agent of Spofford and Tileston, who held a concession to run steamers back and forth from New York with the right to keep five percent of all duties on merchandise carried. Spoffords were the American agents for the British Hartmont loan of 1869, a colossal swindle which will be dealt with later. It was Hartmont who paid Fabens's expenses in Washington as "Dominican Ambassador" at one period in the negotiations for American annexation.[3]

Spofford, Fabens and Cazneau were all stockholders in the National Bank of Santo Domingo, an American concern chartered by Edward Prime, Jr., and Edward Hollister, of New York, "and their associates." The list of these "associates" was never published in full, but it was publicly charged in the newspapers, without provoking libel suits, that high officials of the Dominican Government were included. Prime, who managed the bank, told the United States Commercial Agent that a General sent down by President Grant, who had denied having any investments on the island, was one of the people "interested" in the concern.

The pre-war negotiations for Samana Bay as an Ameri-

THE AMERICAN WEST INDIA COMPANY

can naval station were resumed by Secretary Seward, who had taken a West India cruise for his health in 1866. Cuba was not ripe for intervention just then, and a scheme for annexing the Virgin Islands failed to pass the Senate. The Johnson Administration went out of office during a lull in the Santo Domingo negotiations, but Fabens went to great lengths to interest President Grant and his Cabinet in the project. General Babcock admitted before the Hatch Committee that it was the activities of Fabens at Washington which led to his own first visit for President Grant in 1869.

General Orville E. Babcock had been on Grant's staff during the Civil War, and was later made one of the four secretaries at the Executive Mansion. It was never legally established that the man was dishonest in money matters, though he was repeatedly tried on different charges. Raymond H. Perry, U. S. Commercial Agent in Santo Domingo, accused him of the grossest improprieties, in official letters and statements under oath. Besides Babcock's open association with Cazneau and Fabens, against whom he had been officially warned, evidence was presented to show that he had been responsible for the illegal imprisonment of Davis Hatch in Santo Domingo for fear he would come to the United States and tell what he knew about the financial background of the annexation scheme.

Babcock was sent to Santo Domingo on a warship by President Grant in 1869. Without any instructions from the State Department to do so, he signed a treaty protocol, styling himself as "Aide-de-Camp to His Excellency, Ulysses S. Grant, President of the United States of America." In this document, he agreed that the President would use his political influence to put the treaty through the United States Senate! When accused by Perry of improper economic connections, as well as diplomatic high-handedness, Babcock resorted to an attack upon the author of these charges. Perry's record, as spread before the Committee, showed that a court martial had found him guilty of stealing various army mules and horses during the Civil War, and that failure to drop him from the service had been due to a clerical oversight. Thus the Hatch Investigation lost its dignity for some days, and occupied itself with the question of which man was less to be trusted, the General sent by President Grant to negotiate the annexation treaty, or the Major sent by the State Department to sign it.

In his instructions to Commander Owen of the U.S.S. "Seminole," dated July 15, 1869, the Secretary of the Navy wrote as follows: "You will remain at Samana or on the coast of St. Domingo while General Babcock is there, and give him the moral support of your guns." Lest this "moral support" should prove insufficient in a country where the momentarily successful revolutionary faction was preparing to sell out to a foreign power, another ship was ordered out from Key West August 29. This was the last straw to Senator Charles Sumner, Chairman of the Committee on Foreign Relations in the Senate. He had been the champion of what he considered to be the rights of colored people for decades, and distrusted the smell of the economic background of these annexation proceedings; but the main point to a succession of his powerful speeches before packed galleries is summarized in one sentence:

> "I speak only according to unquestionable reason and the instincts of the human heart when I assert that a contract for the cession of territory must be fair and without suspicion of overawing force."[4]

THE AMERICAN WEST INDIA COMPANY 11

Babcock's protocol had developed in the State Department into two treaties, with their clauses so closely interknit that it is impossible to separate them. The first was a fifty-year lease of the Samana region for a naval base at an annual rental of $150,000. If it passed in both countries, it was to run its course even if annexation failed. The first installment was paid down, $100,000 in cash and the rest in war materials, before either treaty was ratified in either country. With these resources in his hands, President Baez proposed to put the Samana lease through his Congress, without consulting the people. Assured of ample funds for a long period, he would then reverse the process and carry the broader scheme of annexation by arranging a "popular" vote which his forces could control and his Congress would not dare oppose. This game is sometimes known as playing both ends against the middle. The Dominican President objected to any mention of the annexation treaty in the one which he was to present to his Congress, but this proved logically impossible. The advance of $150,000 (the exact amount paid, including war supplies, was $147,229.91) was to be deducted from the $1,500,000 mentioned in the annexation treaty, provided this was ratified.[5]

President Grant's feud with Senator Sumner over San Domingo was only one small part of a tissue of political hatreds which filled this unfortunate Administration in a Reconstruction Period looked back upon with pride by few, if any, Americans. The President stuck to Babcock. In characterizing this man as an obvious liar in the minority Hatch report, Carl Schurz told only a fraction of what was commonly believed about him. When Babcock was indicted for conspiring to defraud the Government in 1876, Grant dismissed the Special

Counsel for the Government and crippled the prosecution. There were various other indictments, but the man either led a charmed life or actually kept within the law, contrary to the common opinion of him. No doubt the legend that Sumner accused Grant himself of corruption was due to the association of a gullible protector with his protégé. Evidence is wanting that such a charge was ever made, even if its supposed author had not testified to the contrary. The President evidently believed that Sumner had promised to support the annexation project. Witnesses to the informal conversation on which this belief rested, supported the Senator's assertion that all he had pledged was "careful consideration," but Grant could never be convinced on this point. He was a man without finesse, and could no more understand Sumner's scruples than the Senator could his chief's complacency about the "great business," as Cazneau called it. President Grant's messages are really astonishing in the smugness with which they allude to the financial returns which he thought his country would get from the adventure.[6]

When it became obvious that the Senate would not accept the treaty, President Grant still refused to acknowledge defeat, turning, instead, to the idea of annexation by a joint resolution, which would require only a simple majority in each house. He proposed to send a commission to Santo Domingo to make arrangements. Thirty senators absented themselves when the vote authorizing the President to appoint such commissioners was taken. The House passed the resolution January 10, 1871, with an ominous amendment to the effect that Congress was in no way committed to annexation thereby. Benjamin F. Wade, Samuel G. Howe and Andrew D. White were appointed. They spent twenty-two days in the capital of Santo Domingo, conferring with a Gov-

THE AMERICAN WEST INDIA COMPANY 13

ernment already publicly committed to annexation, and somewhat less in the remainder of the country. There were no roads worthy of the name, in a mountainous region twice the size of Connecticut, with Massachusetts and Rhode Island thrown in. Even now, with regular steamship services and excellent automobile roads, three weeks would hardly suffice for a thorough tour, let alone studies and surveys. Moreover, their itinerary is a matter of record. Besides missing whole sections of the Republic, they went tearing through what they did see. Andrew D. White crossed from South to North in eleven days, which was just the time required for the mail. The 1871 Commisioners' Report has always been accepted at a good deal more than it could possibly be worth—which is full value for a ridiculously inadequate amount of time consumed.

Sumner's speech of March 27, 1871, was delivered a few days ahead of the submission of this favorable report in print. Annexation was already dead. The Grant Administration did not compromise itself even by bringing about a vote. This whole "great business" of Cazneau's had been a little too mysterious for the Senate. Especially were there too many people in anomalous and indecipherable positions. For instance, Fabens had gone to Washington, at Hartmont's expense, as Dominican Ambassador. He had also visited Santo Domingo at the American Government's expense, to find out the exact amount of the Dominican debt, returning by the next boat with a round figure. This sum did not include the Hartmont loan, then being negotiated, nor did Fabens make any mention of it. Nobody knew, nor does to this day, just what the total of these obligations was; but we were on the point of assuming them. Sumner and some of his fellow Senators could not see it that way.

CHAPTER III

THE SAN DOMINGO IMPROVEMENT COMPANY

Who ever yet discovered, in the anatomy of any corporation, either bowels or a heart?—WILLIAM HONE.

SANTO DOMINGO's worst periods of disorder have never been able entirely to subdue the enthusiasm of foreign investors. Some of the twenty-acre plots which Cazneau dangled before the eyes of freezing New Englanders were as rich as he stated. The eternal summer which he promised actually obtains, and it is true that the highest temperatures would not be considered unusual in many parts of the United States in August. Nevertheless, the American small farmers who went down found it impossible to do much work in the fields. Strange fevers attacked them, unfamiliar pests destroyed their crops, and it proved useless to raise the highly advertised corn fifteen feet tall because there was no market for it. People who have never lived in the tropics or sub-tropics have difficulty in realizing that it is the persistency of fairly high temperatures, not the extremes registered by the thermometer, which saps their energy and puts them on a different physical plane from that possible in one of the temperate zones.

Probably Cazneau's type of colonization could never succeed in Santo Domingo, though the earlier failures did not prevent different people from making similar attempts later. The General himself was perhaps more of an optimist than a villain, underestimating the effects of steady heat on others born in Massachusetts because he was seasoned to it. Like many people before and since, he had read of the shiploads of gold taken from the island by the Spaniards in the early days, and he spent much of his life chasing this particular rainbow. There were two jokers in the game. The Spaniards had secured their gold by demanding it as tribute from the natives, who washed the yellow metal out of the river sands. Gold had a much higher purchasing power in 1500 than in the nineteenth century, when the world supply was vastly greater. Moreover, there was no labor cost to be figured by Spain. Mining has never paid in Santo Domingo since the original natives were exterminated. Prospecting and attempting to farm have ruined many Americans there since 1870. Far more money has been thrown away, however, by sending it to the authors of glowing prospectuses than by attempting operations in person. Perhaps such purchasers have got what they deserved. It is especially hard to keep the fool from parting from his money when the property named in the "investment" is far away and fraud difficult to prove. Wildcat promotions float upon the cupidity of two sets of optimists, one smarter than the other.

Prime and Hollister's old National Bank of 1869 did not live through the foundering of the American annexation project, and the financial troubles which followed that speculative boom. Howe, one of the three Commissioners of 1870, was at the head of a Samana Bay Company which tried to swing the concession the United States Government had failed to take up. Payments fell into arrears, and the Dominican Government which followed that of Baez, the annexationist, declared the rights forfeited. Spofford and Tileston's steamship concession failed to make money, but a new one by the Clyde Line, dating from 1878, founded a fortune. Wholesale trade, as it existed before 1900, was largely in the hands of foreigners—including Italians, Germans, Spaniards and Porto-Ricans, as well as Americans. Juan Sala and Company, New York, exporters, had a partial import monopoly just before the date mentioned above, the President of Santo Domingo being financially interested in it! An American fruit company had a valuable banana plantation at Sosua, on the northern coast.

The two types of foreign economic penetration which were to prove most important in the decades following 1870 were: first, loans to the Government at high interest rates, secured by mortgages of some kind on the country's resources; second, sugar plantations. These loans cannot be discussed in detail, because they would fill a book by themselves; but the outstanding ones will be traced briefly one at a time, beginning with that of Edward H. Hartmont in 1869. The sugar industry, though long prosperous in Cuba and Porto Rico, was introduced into Santo Domingo on a large scale only after the outbreak of the "Ten Years' War" in Cuba in 1868. Cubans founded the first plantations and mills, but Americans and Italians were soon in the lead.

Under the agreement of May 1, 1869, Hartmont and Company were to raise £420,000 by the sale of bonds—£320,000 for the Dominican Government and £100,000, or roughly a half million of dollars, for themselves as commision. Hartmont began deducting his commission at the start. He got the loan listed on the London Stock Exchange by fraud, sold most of the bonds after the Dominican Congress had cancelled the agreement for

THE SAN DOMINGO IMPROVEMENT CO.   17

ample cause—non-fulfillment of terms—and misapplied the greater part of the net sum realized (£372,009 15s. 1d.). Some of this was paid to bondholders as interest on money never received by Santo Domingo, in order to hold the market steady until the issue could be sold; some was held against his own claims for alleged damages to concessions. All told, the Dominican Government got about $190,000, and was asked to pay back nearly $4,000,000, with interest at 6 percent. The price collapsed immediately when the payment of interest from principal was stopped.

Most of the Hartmont bonds were exchanged for those of the next important loan, the Westendorp one of 1888, at the rate of five to one. Nearly all of the rest were purchased at 28 cents on the dollar in 1897, in connection with a loan arranged by the San Domingo Improvement Company, an American concern which succeeded Westendorp. Two sets of bonds were financed by Westendorp and Company, of Amsterdam: the first, in 1888, for £770,000, and the second in 1890 for £900,000. The latter was to cover a contract with Van Den Tex Bondt for the construction of a railway from Puerta Plata to Santiago de los Caballeros. Westendorp was given a supervision over the Dominican custom houses which seems to have been planned after the regime then in force in Egypt, but lacked the international sanctions of the latter. Both bond issues went into default in 1892.

Westendorp was ruined. At first he tried through American attorneys, Smith M. Weed and Messrs. Brown and Wells, to sell his bonds and custom house rights in Santo Domingo to the United States Government. When this attempt failed, the three American lawyers organized the San Domingo Improvement Company to take over the Westendorp interests. It was incorporated in New Jersey in 1892, and drew up a new convention which was ratified by the Dominican Congress, March 24, 1893. After a lapse of two decades, America had again become the leading foreign actor on the Dominican stage. The American economic grip upon Santo Domingo was much tighter in 1893 than any brief sketch can indicate. We must remember the Clyde steamship monopoly, and the tremendous growth of the sugar industry. A French *Banque Nationale de Saint Domingue* had been organized in 1889. It got into a quarrel with the Dominican Government, and French intervention was threatened. Under these circumstances, the San Domingo Improvement Company bought it out at the request of President Heureaux. The whole series of bonds slumped in the market in 1897 when one issue went into default. A new issue floated by the Improvement Company was no luckier than the previous ones. Currency depreciation was resorted to, and the Dominican Government became practically bankrupt.[1]

At the end of the complicated refunding operations in 1897 the bonded debt of Santo Domingo stood at £3,885,350. Of this total, over two-thirds was in 2¾ percent obligations, the rest drawing 4 percent. The new unified loan went into default April 1, 1899, and President Heureaux, practical dictator for nearly two decades, was assassinated July 26 of that year. After this, affairs moved haltingly but surely toward foreclosure. The question of the bonded indebtedness was vastly complicated by floating obligations of various sorts and uncertain amounts, claims held largely by merchant-bankers and other business men resident in the country but of foreign nationality.

President J. I. Jimenez, who succeeded Heureaux,

made an agreement with the Improvement Company in
1900, practically putting this concern in charge of customs collections. This was repudiated by the Belgian
bondholders, and later by the other European ones excepting the British. The bulk of the bonds had been
marketed in Europe. While the Improvement Company
claimed to have received authorization to act for a majority, in the final line-up after the split it was left with
a minority claim. Governments began to act in support
of their own citizens, the private customs receivership
broke down completely, and the general result was hopeless confusion. The Dominican Government dealt separately with the European bondholders. Public opinion
in Santo Domingo was almost solidly hostile to the Improvement Company, which had amassed large claims
with the expenditure of relatively little actual money.
Small holders, mainly in Europe, who had paid cash for
bonds, in good faith, were the real victims. Such of
their money as had not been stolen, misappropriated, or
paid out in ridiculous commissions, salaries and bribes,
had finally disappeared in mismanaged improvement
schemes or worse ventures, such as military preparations.
The Improvement Company was thoroughly hated in
Santo Domingo as the favorite tool of a vanished despotism. Negotiations in 1901 came to nothing, as the
Dominican Congress insisted that the Company's claims
must be settled in the courts of the Republic. The State
Department wanted to act unofficially, hoping that
Santo Domingo might buy out the Improvement Company. Besides public and parliamentary opposition, the
fact that the Dominican Government could not raise the
money was an insuperable obstacle to this kind of a
settlement.

On January 6, 1902, the San Domingo Improvement

Company appealed a second time to the State Department, filing a brief and asking for intervention. Nineteen items were set down in a list of claims totaling $11,000,000. American intervention was coming, but the evil day was put off. Vice-President Abbott of the Improvement Company was sent to Santo Domingo to work with the American Minister for a settlement. French and Belgian claims had been scaled down about a third in a settlement of 1901. As usual, the entire customs revenue was pledged, the income of the ports of Santo Domnigo and San Pedro de Marcoris (the outlet of the great sugar district) being specifically mentioned. This independent settlement with European claimants completely demoralized the machinery for collection under international sanction mentioned in the Improvement Company's contract of 1893. It is hard to imagine what the French and Belgians could have been thinking about, unless they assumed that their governments would intervene when the time came, and that the United States would do nothing at all. They seem to have overlooked the fact that a Spanish-American war had taken place, and that we had begun collecting a colonial empire. If they could have looked forward a year to President Roosevelt's "firm and dextrous" angling for the Canal Zone, as a British writer tartly put it, their ideas might have taken a different turn.

On January 31, 1903, a protocol was signed whereby the Dominican Government was to pay over to the United States Government, for the San Domingo Improvement Company, the sum of $4,500,000 in American gold. The terms and method of payment were to be fixed by two arbitrators named by the Presidents of the Republics and a third named by these two. All the

THE SAN DOMINGO IMPROVEMENT CO. 21

Company's rights, properties and claims were to be ceded to the Dominican Government. This was the end of the private receivership of 1888 and 1893. The foreign creditors of Santo Domingo had acquired the right to look to their Governments for collection. This was disputed for a time, on the ground that the short-lived Vasquez Government, responsible for it, was obviously an illegal dictatorship, but the Americans forced successive governments to acknowledge the acts of their predecessors until the claim was made good. One payment of $18,750 was made on the Improvement Company account in February, 1903, and that was all.

A successful revolution occurred in April and another in November. In December, the arbitral commission met. It finally decided[2] on July 14, 1904, that the Dominican Government must pay the Improvement Company award at the rate of $37,500 a month for two years, and $41,666 a month afterward. A financial agent named by the United States Government was to take over the Puerto Plata custom-house if the payment of any month were not forthcoming. The remaining northern custom-houses—Monte Cristi, Samana and Sanchez—were to follow if the first one did not produce the money.

Nobody who will read the briefs in the case can have a shadow of doubt as to the idea in the minds of the American Commissioners. Santo Domingo could not raise the money, and the Puerto Plata custom-house was taken over in October, 1904, as expected. The French followed the American example in December, threatening to take over the Santo Domingo custom-house, which would have paralyzed the Government at once. Italy had already made an armed gesture by sending her

Minister at Havana over in a warship to negotiate. To avoid this financial partitioning of the country, the Dominican Government made an eleventh-hour proposal that the United States establish a customs receivership for the entire Republic. This was not a free and spontaneous move, but a bid for common bondage as the alternative to dismemberment.

To the student of economic imperialism, the most interesting thing in these negotiations is the bold argument from the "Egyptian precedent" by the agent of the United States.[3] He went to great lengths to show the similarities of the two cases, quoting British authorities on the benefits which had accrued to Egypt from the intervention, and dwelling with special affection upon that "cornerstone of English influence," the Financial Adviser. Anybody who will read the earlier drafts of the conventions for establishing an official American customs receivership, and especially the despatches of Minister Dawson and Commander Dillingham concerning the negotiations, in the 1905 volume of *Foreign Relations*, can see at a glance how profoundly saturated were the minds of these two men with the "Egyptian precedent." We do not have to surmise anything—they expressed themselves clearly enough. Egypt was not specifically mentioned in the 1907 negotiations or convention. That the idea remained is obvious enough from the fact that the State Department tried repeatedly after the troubles of 1911-12 to read the right to demand a financial adviser into the actual terms of the 1907 Convention.

The American Commissioners in the arbitration of 1904 deliberately paved the way to a partial receivership, almost but not quite private, under the Vice-President

THE SAN DOMINGO IMPROVEMENT CO.   23

of the Improvement Company. This provoked international complications which led to the semi-official American receivership of 1905, in a way to be pointed out in the next chapter. The semi-official receivership of 1905 led directly to the official one of 1907. Nine years later, after a long dispute as to whether the 1907 document gave the American Government the right to install a financial adviser (nowhere mentioned in its text), the United States Marines "pacified" Santo Domingo, and a Military Government was set up when the Dominicans still refused to follow the "Egyptian precedent."

Joaquin Delgado, a Cuban, built the first large steam sugar mill in Santo Domingo in 1874, on the *La Esperanza* plantation, near the capital. A smaller one had been erected already by another Cuban, Charles Loynaz, on the San Marcos River near Puerto Plata. The success of these men inspired two of their fellow-Cubans to follow their example. E. Lamar set up the *La Caridad* mill at San Carlos, west of the capital, and Juan Amechazurra founded *La Angelina* near San Pedro de Macoris in the southeastern part of the republic. This is the great sugar district, and *Angelina* is still one of the larger mills and plantations. A little later, Padron y Solaun founded *Consuelo,* also near Macoris and at this writing (1927) the second largest in Santo Domingo. The last property was acquired by Alexander Bass, and this American family has been identified with it, in one way or another, ever since.[4]

Macoris was made a port of entry in 1880. The region was erected into a "Maritime District" in 1882 and made a province in 1908. By this time it was the most concentrated center of wealth in the country—a wealth which was mainly foreign. The sugar output of the entire republic in 1880 was around 8,000,000 pounds, or roughly 7 percent of the 1905 crop. In 1882, there were 16 sugar mills in operation on the south side of the island, and 12 more under construction. Not all of these survived the severe beet-sugar competition between this time and the end of the century. The crop of 1883 rose to 17,000,000 pounds, or about 17 percent of the 1905 yield. By 1886 the output had passed 35,000,000 pounds, a figure to be tripled by 1905, by which time an average crop would run over 100,000,000 pounds.[5]

Sugar was in national and international politics from the start. It was in Dominican politics to keep from paying export, production and (later) land taxes. The American and Italian Governments were also used when possible for protection of their citizens or the companies organized under their laws, and to keep the tariff walls as low as might be. For example, the planters subscribed $18,000 in May, 1884, to aid the Dominican Government in sending a commission to the United States to work for a reciprocity treaty.

From the start, the sugar industry was founded upon cheap Dominican land and cheap West India labor. Dominican laborers were not plentiful enough—at least at the wages offered—to supply the rapidly increasing demand. Hence a type of black laborer not wanted by the Dominicans as a permanent settler was imported from Haiti and the British West Indies. His presence was a damper upon the normal growth of the native population, kept out more desirable immigrants, and tended to hold wages down. Peasants were not tempted by the low rates of pay to leave their small plots, and a country of small farmers is peculiarly unadapted to the

THE SAN DOMINGO IMPROVEMENT CO.

cane-sugar industry. The experience with it in Haiti of recent years furnishes rather startling evidence of this. In a word, sugar planting, as established in Santo Domingo at the opening of our century, could not grow without doing conscious or unconscious violence to the social and economic life of the country. And it grew.

CHAPTER IV

PRESIDENT ROOSEVELT'S TWO RECEIVERSHIPS

> I put the agreement into effect, and I continued its execution for two years before the Senate acted, and I would have continued it until the end of my term, if necessary, without any action by Congress.—THEODORE ROOSEVELT

NOTHING has been more carefully guarded in discussing the negotiations between the United States and Santo Domingo than the legal fiction that a bedevilled Dominican Government freely asked and was generously granted our assistance. President Roosevelt, referring to the 1905 Protocol, wrote:[1] "The treaty now before the Senate was concluded with Santo Domingo's earnest request repeatedly pressed upon us, and was submitted to the Senate because in my judgment it was our duty to our less fortunate neighbor to respond to her call for aid." The American official version thus far does not clearly misstate the facts which it chooses to employ. That it falsifies by omitting some of them is perhaps because the whole truth would have marred the legend of our chivalrous altruism.

The "call for aid" was heard after United States Minister Dawson, in compliance with a telegram from Secretary of State Hay (December 30, 1904),[2] sounded the President of Santo Domingo to "ascertain whether his Government would be disposed to request the United

States to take charge of the collection of duties and effect an equitable distribution of the assigned quotas among the Dominican Government and the several claimants." Dawson telegraphed back that the Dominican President was "disposed" to make this "request" on condition that 40 percent of the annual customs receipts should be distributed among all the creditors, and the remaining 60 percent turned over to his Government. He also wanted assurance that no official of the Improvement Company should be allowed to act as Financial Agent.

The next step was to get terms satisfactory to us and to phrase them so carefully that they would be constitutionally accepted in both countries. Commander Dillingham of the United States Navy was sent to aid Minister Dawson in this task. The European Claimants would evidently accept whatever line of action we decided upon. They merely wanted their money, while we wanted both our money and our Monroe Doctrine. That Roosevelt had any real intention of permitting other foreign powers to occupy any new ports in the Carribean is hardly to be supposed.[3] His politeness to the Italians might easily have meant no more than that their threats suited his own purposes by having a moral effect both upon the Dominicans whom he was yearning to protect and upon the United States Senators whose permission he would have to secure.

There was no need for the two Americans to worry President Morales with doubts that the United States Senate would agree to the "generous" action. The Dominican President, on his part, was no less eager to get a protocol signed before his own Congress or people should have any chance for united opposition. Minister Dawson explained to him in the course of a later conversation that he had "appreciated the reasons which had induced him not to raise the question of the necessity for ratification, and well understood that his only hope to prevent a revolution had been immediately to present the matter to the excited country as an accomplished fact, thus leaving the malcontents confronted with the alternative of undertaking a hopeless fight for which they had no chance to prepare themselves, or of submitting without resistance." [4]

Dillingham and Dawson made the first draft of the protocol and signed it, January 20, 1905, before the text had been submitted as a whole to Washington. It was the financial machinery actually set up by these men which was important, however, not the words which they put on paper. Santo Domingo was to get 45 percent of the revenues, and her creditors 55 percent, less the cost of collection. The receivership was to have a free hand in the custom-houses and the power to preserve order. At the moment of signing the original draft, the American negotiators had been obliged to insert in the preamble a clause "guaranteeing the complete integrity of the territory of the Dominican Republic." It is almost an article of faith today in Santo Domingo that only by such rigid insistence upon constitutional guarantees was their country later spared the lot of Haiti.

What was really in the minds of the two American negotiators was to copy British rule in Egypt. In a long letter[5] explaining their original draft, Minister Dawson called the attention of the State Department to a clause in Article III, in which the Dominican Government agreed "to keep its administrative expenditures within the limits of the indispensable necessities of administration." If this had gone through, it would have formed a perfect excuse for American intervention at will. As Dawson explained, it "opens the door to a real superintendence of all administrative matters, which in wise hands can be used to great advantage. Its practical effect can be made like that of similar clauses in the financial agreements to which the Government of Egypt is a party." The State Department did not see fit to risk presenting the clause to the Senate in the final draft of the 1905 Protocol, and nothing like it appeared in the 1907 Convention. Nevertheless, the American Government was destined, years later, to hunt legal excuses in the text the Senate finally adopted, for sending down a financial advisor. Santo Domingo's refusal to submit to such supervision was to lead to the military occupation of 1916. Might lends extraordinary advantages in the interpretation of legal phrases.

While waiting for the ratification of the agreement,[6] it was necessary to find some workable scheme for financing the Dominican Government, for no one would advance money with the protocol pending. Minister Dawson found a temporary intermediary in the person of Mr. Santiago Michelena, a Porto Rican merchant, and thus an American citizen through the conquest of 1898. He took over the Dominican Government's right to collect the customs revenues (excepting at Puerto Plata, where the Improvement Company was installed), agreeing to pay the employees, who were to be responsible to him. Beginning with February 1, 1905, he was to hand over to the Dominican Government $75,000 per month, and to hold the balance in trust. Sums due him were to draw interest at 6 percent. His compensation was to be a 2 percent commission for the collection of the $75,000 monthly, and 1 percent for its transfer, which would amount in a year to $27,000. The revenues were estimated at $110,000 a month, thus making an additional $35,000 subject to his fees, as fixed by himself and the American Minister. When Desiderio Arias, Governor of the practically independent province of Monte Cristi, did not take kindly to this plan, he was persuaded to comply at an interview with Admiral Sigsbee on an American warship, in the course of which the Admiral mentioned that Monte Cristi would be held "responsible" for any action contrary to the protocol. Governor Arias knew what this meant, so he turned his custom-house over to an American naval officer.

When, on March 18, the United States Senate adjourned without taking action on this protocol, the foreign powers renewed their demands and inquiries, and the Dominican Minister of Finance asked Dawson to "indicate some practical modus vivendi pending ratification." The latter finally suggested that his Government might find somebody to take charge of a customs receivership if formally requested to do so. He found President Morales primed with this very same idea. Next Dawson saw the Italian representative, who, he stated, was evidently expecting him. The others were more surprised but hardly less friendly to the scheme. They were willing to accept a suspension of payments pending ratification, and some of them pointedly suggested that the Improvement Company do likewise. President Roosevelt had just sent Dr. Jacob H. Hollander as his confidential agent to investigate matters, and the Improvement Company's claim was included with the rest.

Accordingly, on March 31, President Morales issued a decree[7] setting up a modus vivendi receivership on the following day. Colonel George R. Colton, who had seen long service in the Philippine custom-houses, was appointed chief collector. Forty-five percent of the revenue was to be paid to the Dominican Government, and the remainder was to be deposited in the National City Bank of New York. It was made clear in the telegram of the acting Secretary of State to Minister Dawson that this was a temporary arrangement, to be proclaimed as the Dominican Republic's own plan. The form of a protocol must be avoided, for this, as everyone was aware, would be flatly illegal without the consent of the Senate, whereas the plan adopted was only dubiously legal.

If either the Dominicans or the European creditors had suspected that this "temporary" agreement was to stretch over a period of two years, it would have been impossible to arrange it. But something had to be done to tide over the period of delay, and to make those people and Michelena easy in their minds. Furthermore, the fact that the two presidents were skating on the thin edges of their constitutions had much to do with the flexibility of the plan adopted, and the small amount of friction with which it worked. A few American experts were superimposed upon the old personnel, nobody lost his job, all danger of European intervention (if it had existed) was removed, and internal revolution was checked because the Government had the revenues with which to defend itself. It was the continental European creditors who had won a victory. After all, why should they go to the trouble of fishing their own chestnuts out of the fire, when by keeping the Americans excited they might get it done for them? The main sufferers were the creditors in the Improvement Company. When Roosevelt saw that he had to coerce them into surrendering their advantages under the 1904 arbitration award, there was no hesitation. The claim was finally scaled down 10 percent, which the British holders regarded as a base betrayal of their interests.

As it appeared in 1905, the joke was on the American Senate. Many of its members regarded President Roosevelt's modus vivendi in Santo Domingo as a gross breach of courtesy and propriety, if not an illegal extension of his privileges under the Constitution. The particular protocol "pending" had been designed to operate as a treaty. Thus, insofar as the modus vivendi set up the machinery and subserved the functions contemplated, it took the place of a treaty. The difficulty of withdrawing the receivership, once established, gave the "big stick" a formidable weight it would not have had otherwise. This use of an executive agreement to create accomplished facts with which to coerce the Senate was an innovation highly distasteful to that body.

According to Roosevelt's own account,[8] we are asked to believe that a few pacifists, devoted to prattle and the cult of inefficiency, and casually allied with a handful of "reactionaries" and "Democrats" in the Senate, held up the true evangel of peace and progress, without "a single sound reason of any kind." He, the real apostle of international peace, armed to the teeth, laid down his own crushing argument thus: "The Constitution did not explicitly give me the power to bring about the necessary agreement with Santo Domingo. But the Constitution did not forbid me to do what I did." According to this interpretation, the President has a right to do anything for preventing which no adequate machinery is provided. Actually, the Senate steadfastly refused to ratify the "pending" protocol for nearly two years, and finally forced its replacement with a "convention" more in line with its own ideas.

The entire economic system of the smallest country

is an extremely complicated piece of machinery—far more so than a mere business which turns over the same amount of money a year. In the case of the modus vivendi in Santo Domingo, the sending of half the public revenue to New York, where it was held for creditors, was certain to affect private business profoundly. American dollars were adopted as the standard currency in June, 1905, and the native pieces stabilized at one-fifth of face value. This move of course stimulated the demand for American money. It is also obvious that those payments into the creditors' fund in New York represented products of Dominican soil and labor, sold abroad for sums which did not come back to Santo Domingo in any form.

A great deal of political capital was made by Americans of the enormous "favorable" trade balance of the Dominican Republic. During the calendar year 1905, the exports were valued at $6,880,890, and the imports at only $2,736,828. The "favorable" balance of $4,144,062 was so large, in fact, as to be ruinous. Practically half of the entire value of exports was sugar, which was almost purely a foreign industry. Ninety-eight percent of the $3,292,470 worth exported in 1905 went to the United States. Some of the money was paid to manufacturers of machinery, and some went to the Clyde Line for transportation costs. What interest was paid on investments went chiefly to Americans or Italians. Even the wages paid to laborers were collected almost entirely by foreigners—British West Indians or Haitians—and the salaried personnel was also mainly foreign. Outside the sugar industry things were not so bad, but the largest cacao business was owned by a Swiss chocolate manufacturer, and the one large fruit plantation by an American concern.[9]

Practically the entire revenue of the State was collected from the small figure of $2,736,828 for imports, while the nearly seven millions of dollars for exports went largely to foreign investors abroad, and paid almost no taxes. The high duties on imported manufactures did not hurt the American producers, who simply added them to the prices of their goods. The burden fell on the Dominican consumers, who were particularly poor. It is true that the Dominican Government's 45 percent share of the revenues netted more than the whole in previous years, but what is less apparent is that the nation, in getting more money to run its government, was doing so at the expense of sending an even greater amount of purchasing power out of the country.

In 1905 there was hardly more than a beginning of the vast web of American business that was to grow up later in the shadow of the customs receivership, with its tariff readjustments, and especially under the protection of the Military Government. The one great American commercial enterprise at that time was the Clyde steamship monopoly. In 1878, the Government of Santo Domingo had granted it freedom from all duties and port charges, and 3 ½ percent of the duty on the imports and exports it carried. This was never paid, and the Clyde line kept remitting the balance due in exchange for extensions of its concession. In 1895 it gave up the right to this 3 ½ percent and forgave the arrears in compensation for the provision that all other companies were to pay the tonnage and port charges, which were not to be lowered. Thus Clyde could charge the most exorbitant rates because he was exempt from the heavy Government charges that his competitors had to pay. The celebrated *Cherokee* case of 1903, in which under American naval guns the rights of the Clyde Line were placed above the right of the Dominican Government to protect its existence, broke off all friendly relations between the steamship company and the country on which it lived. In 1906 the Dominican Minister of Finance attempted to reduce the port charges in an effort to remove some of the handicap to foreign trade. He argued that the rates had originally been fixed in Mexican silver, and therefore had been automatically doubled by the change to gold. The Clyde Company answered that this doubling was merely a part of the consideration they received for canceling their 3½ percent subsidy, and the American Minister backed their position. Since there were suits pending against two other American concerns at the same time, Dawson suggested to the Dominican President that it would be unadvisable to let the impression become general that his Government was adverse to all American enterprise, and the matter was dropped. The monopoly disappeared when the 1907 Convention went into force.

A land tax in the Dominican Republic was impracticable, first because there was too much vacant land, and second because of the prevalence of *peso* or collective titles, under which one man could hold a certain share of a large area. Correct assessment under such a system was impossible. The general survey necessary to establish, guarantee, and register titles had not yet been made twenty years after 1905, and was still considered beyond the Government's means.

The one promising source of the export balance which was necessary to pay foreign creditors was sugar. Therefore the temptation of any foreign collection agency to become friendly with the industry in order to make a showing was irresistible. In the preceding chapter we have sketched its extent. At the end of 1903,

Morales sold the planters exemption from the tax of a cent a pound for twenty years. The next year, however, a decree was passed declaring the tax in force, but no collections were made during that year. At the beginning of 1905, the Government decided to enforce the tax, and collect arrears as well, claiming that the exemption was unconstitutional. The planters refused to pay, and the American Department of State, when appealed to, delayed matters until the test case of William Bass, an American, came up before the Supreme Court of Santo Domingo. In May, 1906, it was decided in favor of the Government. The Morales decree was declared invalid and unenforceable because it had attempted to limit the action of subsequent legislative bodies. Bass was presented with a bill for $24,000. He appealed again to the American Minister, thus opening a new series of negotiations which were later suspended, pending the new Convention. In the meantime, April 20, 1906, the Dominican Congress passed a law exempting sugar from taxation after August first of that year. Thus expired the Dominican Government's last efficacious means of taxing the one great export industry.[10]

The sugar exports alone in 1905 amounted to $3,292,470 or $555,642 more than the total imports, which paid the taxes. Moreover the growth of this industry choked the development of a better balanced agriculture, which might have cultivated wheat, corn, cacao, and coffee. This one industry belonged to foreigners, collected from the fertility of over 30,000 acres of land, shipped out the product free of taxes, and made money abroad for its owners, much of which never came back in any form to Santo Domingo. This explains in a measure the harshness toward American interests so marked in the country.

Another reason was the fact that nearly a million dollars of the country's money was tied up in the National City Bank in New York, waiting upon a seemingly endless wrangle between the American President and Senate. The moratorium under the modus vivendi, like the Biblical rain, fell alike upon the just and the unjust. It forced the small and honest claimants as well as the larger and sometimes more doubtful ones, to wait interminably for their money. On the whole, the big foreign creditors, protected by international agreements, fared better than the people at home. The two years' wait, during which creditors grew sick and tired of collecting nothing, played no small part in the reduction of the debt.

On May 19, 1906, Dawson wrote a letter to Secretary Root in which he expressed alarm because of the hampering of commercial relations by the export of currency. In June it was decided to send Ministers Velasquez and Tejera to Washington. During the next three months, these gentlemen, in conference or correspondence with senators, creditors, financiers and others in the United States, agreed upon the substance of what was to become the 1907 Convention.

The grand total of the Dominican debt had originally amounted, with interest, to about $40,000,000. Most of the interest had been thrown out immediately. Through proposal and counter-proposal, the remaining foreign claims had been scaled down from $21,407,000 to $12,407,000. Internal debts of about $2,028,258 were adjusted at about $645,827, and the remainder of unliquidated odds and ends brought the whole to around $17,000,000. A plan for arriving at these sums was sent to the creditors in the name of the Dominican Government early in September, 1906, and thus the

American State Department got rid of all responsibility, although its agent, Dr. Hollander, had done the job. While this settlement was supposedly arrived at by mutual agreement, the "agreement" was by no means free from pressure. Some Italian claimants refused to accept the amount arbitrarily set aside for them, as did also the British who had bought through the Improvement Company. The latter, who, it is estimated, lost about $150,000 in principal and interest by the cut, were the more firmly convinced they had been sold out when the fact became known that Dr. Hollander had collected $100,000 from the Dominican Government in December, 1908. On August 1, the State Department had paid him in full for his services during a period of two years and ten months, the sum being $32,500. The simple facts of the transaction seemed to show that he had then taken $100,000 from a bankrupt government for less than four and a half months in which he did nothing at all. Hollander's own explanation was that this sum was a sort of retainer for his services, "for all eternity" if necessary, after August 1, 1908.[11]

Kuhn, Loeb and Company were willing to float a loan of $20,000,000 for 50 years at 5 percent, the Morton Trust Company to act as depository and fiscal agent. When the 1907 Convention was finally ratified, the accumulation in cash resulting from the modus vivendi amounted to over $3,000,000. Added to the $3,000,000 by which the loan exceeded the national debt, this made a handsome sum available for buying up onerous concessions and beginning public improvements.

What the Convention actually did[12] was to install a General Receiver of Dominican Customs, Assistant Receivers and other employees of the receivership appointed by the President of the United States. These appointees were to collect all the customs duties and to pay them out in the following order:

1. Receivership expenses—not to exceed 5 percent of the total, except by agreement between the two governments;
2. Interest upon the bonds;
3. Amortization—including interest on bonds held in sinking fund;
4. Purchase and cancellation of bonds, according to their terms or as directed by the Dominican Government;
5. Remainder to go to the Dominican Government.

A minimum of $100,000 per month, or $1,200,000 per year, was to be deposited in a New York bank for the creditors. If the revenues should exceed $3,000,000 during any year, one half of the surplus was to go into the sinking fund for the redemption of bonds. Since collections usually exceeded the stipulated amount by a considerable margin, the percentage actually received was more favorable to the Dominican Government than the 45-55 percent apportionment of the modus vivendi period of 1905-07.

Competent European authorities[18] often classified our arrangement with Santo Domingo as a protectorate or a "financial protectorate." Even if we define the word "protectorate" as loosely as possible, it is still difficult to find one in the *text* of the 1907 Convention, which was made vague in order to pass the American Senate and a suspicious Dominican Congress. It was a "fair weather" instrument, and when the first real test came, it had to be either bolstered up or abandoned.

CHAPTER V

THE FAILURE OF THE ROOSEVELT POLICY

And the rain descended, and the floods came, and the winds blew, and beat upon that house; and it fell; and great was the fall thereof.—JESUS OF NAZARETH

FREDERICO VELASQUEZ H., Minister of Finance and Commerce, had that quality, so useful in statesmen, of being able to recognize stark necessity at sight. In the preliminary negotiations of 1905, his measured opposition on all the vital points had at one time irritated the State Department into suggesting an attempt to get rid of him. Minister Dawson had hastily replied that this would never go down with the Dominicans. Velasquez is one of the occasional men whose intelligence commands the respect of a whole country, but who lack the theatrical quality to fire the popular imagination and allay the shade of fear and repugnance which superior minds commonly arouse. For a quarter of a century he has been a great factor in public life, without ever quite reaching the presidency.

In the final arrangements for the 1907 convention, he recognized his own limited technical knowledge, employed expert counsel, asked more than he expected, gave just what ground he had to without any unnecessary fuss, and listened with calm but intensely digestive intelligence to the explanations of why more could not be granted. He was the one Dominican who came

nearest to knowing exactly what he was doing. Since
the risk seemed necessary, it did not count. Men of
action are like that. His colleague, Emiliano Tejera,
Minister of Foreign Affairs, though not as able as Velasquez,
knew how to give his convictions the form and
color demanded by the popular mind. Tejera had to
have something like moral enthusiasm for what he did.
Their reports for the calendar year 1906[1] contain the
real arguments to the Dominican people for accepting
the arrangement just made in Washington and New
York.

Velasquez argued, without wasting a word, that it
was the only practical solution under the circumstances.
Tejera adroitly covered up the fact that it was a political
stroke for their party, assuring it a long lease of
power, and accused opponents of "purely political opposition."
To lay the spectre of American imperialism,
he called the United States the "natural protector of
the weak Spanish-American republics," using Roosevelt's
own illustration of Cuba:

> "Honest man that I am, I must believe the statements
> of honest men of other countries, and I have
> no right to doubt the sincerity of those who, having
> control of Cuba—a hundred times richer than
> our country, a hundred times more governable—
> volunteered to retire and raised her to the rank of
> a sovereign nation. . . ."[2]

Tejera touched most of the main points which had
been raised by the opposition. The Americans had made
deep wounds by their tactlessness in dealing with the
color line. American companies had aroused enmity
or suspicion by trying to get out of paying taxes, by
using imported labor, and by dealing with the Executive

behind the back of Congress. Nothing could be said about the obvious fact that the negotiations for the proposed convention had been carried on in much the same way, so it was not mentioned. Grant's annexation project had never been forgotten, and the San Domingo Improvement Company was still blamed by many for the whole trouble. The one idea which Tejera resolutely combated was that the disturbing chain of events formed an ascending series, with a possible American intervention or annexation at the end, and Cuba was the key argument. In adopting the Convention, after months of debate, the Dominican Congress appended four "explanatory clauses," stating precisely what the body understood to be the meaning of the first two articles, which seemed to some members unpleasantly vague.

There is no clear evidence that anybody saw the greatest weakness of the 1907 Convention, which lay in Article III, not the two complained of. Santo Domingo agreed not to increase her "public debt" or "modify" the import duties until the whole amount of the bonds had been paid, without first convincing the American President that the collections for two years past would have exceeded two million dollars annually at the proposed rates. Does "modify" mean "decrease" in an agreement meant to guarantee a certain minimum volume of receipts, or does it mean "change," thus excluding increases also? Is the "public debt" of a country its *bonded* debt, as the expression is commonly used in languages of Latin derivation, or, as the Americans later insisted, does it also include the floating obligations which most governments incur at times in emergencies? Every agreement printed in two languages is likely to encounter such obstacles in its interpretation.

A great crisis like an armed insurrection would have to be met somehow. When the Dominican Government faced this exact situation after 1911, it was to suspend the payment of salaries and current expenses for a time. Did this constitute an increase in the "public debt," and thus a violation of the terms of the convention? The Americans said yes and the Dominicans no, the latter basing their contention on innumerable passages from treatises on international law in romance languages, the former finally backing theirs with the force of bayonets.

Dominican opposition to the Convention, which was very active in 1907-8, gradually died down. Two years under the Modus Vivendi had already brought reforms in the rules and methods of collection.[3] Rigorous enforcement brought hardship to many, as the old rates had been ridiculously high, mitigated by exemption and corruption. The Americans proposed to reform the tariff entirely, but the new law was not ready for application until the end of 1909. Revenues had steadily increased under the Modus Vivendi, from two and a half millions during the first year to over three the next. The first Convention year, beginning August 1, 1907, set a new record of $3,645,794.79. They fell off somewhat after this, though not dangerously. Another new record was achieved during the revolutionary troubles of 1911-12, and still another the next year, at the height of the insurrection. Dominicans have always insisted that the seriousness of these revolutions has been exaggerated abroad, and it would seem to be demonstrated that at least business was not very seriously dislocated.

The new tariff law finished and passed in 1909 went into effect January 1, 1910.[4] Some concessions were made to Dominican wishes for protection, in order to establish industries at home. On the whole, however, the assumption was that Santo Domingo would import the manufactured goods she needed. Though no blunt discriminations were made, the American drafters were too human not to rejoice that an "impetus was given the importation of many manufactured articles of American origin." Among the articles which came in greater volume were noted: automobiles, typewriters, cash registers, phonographs, platform scales, structural materials, builders' hardware, drugs, chemicals, medicines, paints, machinery and machine parts, tools, furniture, and leather goods. Some of these are not exactly necessities of life, and others could very well have been produced on the ground, given a little initial encouragement. Why should Santo Domingo, long famous for her cattle, import so many shoes and other leather goods? With one of the largest assortments of fine woods on earth, why import her furniture from the United States? The Americans themselves, after occupying Haiti, on the same island, had a great deal of their furniture manufactured there with convict labor, thus getting a kind of mahogany stuff hardly available elsewhere in the world.

This tariff was obviously drawn up with the main idea of getting revenue and making a showing for the foreign receivership. Any American abroad, especially if he is connected with both finance and government, is also likely to bestow some patriotic thought on foreign trade. The health of Dominican industry was thus the least of three principal considerations, and the consumer got rather a rough deal. Professor Fred R. Fairchild, of Yale University, was brought by the American Military Government to Santo Domingo during the winter of 1917-18, to report on the whole system of public finance and make recommendations. At that time, the American-made tariff had been in effect eight years, and had been plastered with encomiums in the annual reports of its designers. Professor Fairchild[5] found little to praise in the system whereby the Receivership had been raising about ten dollars per capita in a country where, as he put it, "most of the people are distinctly poor, having barely enough to support a decidedly low standard of living." In his opinion, the customs duties were levied mainly on necessities, the rates "in many cases fully up to what the traffic will bear, or beyond," and the tendency of the whole mechanism was to "hamper business and check industry." The taxation system, he thought, was "one of the causes of the country's backward economic development."

As the foreign sugar properties grew and became more valuable, their proprietors worried increasingly about the insecurity of the collective (*peso, comunero*) titles. In the early days, the Spanish Government had made big land grants, their boundaries following such natural features as rivers and mountain ranges. Santo Domingo was then mainly a grazing country, there were few fences, and it was important that each holder should have access to water. For these and other reasons, including Spanish law and the comparative solidarity of families, the heirs to lands rarely made physical divisions of the property. The *value*, represented by shares or *pesos* (literally "dollars' worth") was apportioned instead. Land became extremely plentiful as population declined with the opening up of Spain's highly valuable territories on the mainland. As a result, a man would own a certain small share of the title to a big tract. If he wished to farm, he marked out and claimed up to the amount of his share in any unoccupied part. No other title-holder could take this plot as long as he continued to use it. If he let his occupancy lapse, he still had his share in the whole.

This system of land holding bears the earmarks of derivation from one used by the ancient Romans in colonizing various parts of the western Mediterranean region, where vestiges of it still remain. The idea of making use rather than paper titles the basis of claims to particular surfaces has its merits. It was strengthened by the Mohammedans who followed the Romans in the Western Mediterranean, including Spain. Of late years, some Frenchmen have come to the rescue of the general Moslem notion of "live" and "dead" lands which their country has tried so assiduously to destroy in North Africa for generations; but of course it would have to be adapted to modern conditions. The main idea is that a purely speculative title, unaccompanied by use, may be detrimental to the public, and should be at the disposal of the state.

Like the French invaders of North Africa, the Americans could see nothing but a barbarous anachronism in a system of titles based partially on use. In Santo Domingo, the continuous occupier for thirty years could get a permanent title by proving this and complying with certain other conditions. Recurrent disorders and glaring flaws in the registration system had reduced land-holding to something approaching chaos. A law of 1885 had waived the required thirty years of continuous occupation, and taken possession at the time as the basis of title. New revolutions occurred, however, and no adequate recording system was created. Record books were lost or destroyed, false titles were manufactured, and many people had no definite deeds of any kind to their property. Notaries were often corrupted. A law of 1907 forbade the alienation of *comunero* lands without a survey by a licensed public surveyor, but it did not work, and was repealed in 1911.[6] It was now made possible for any shareholder or co-proprietor to demand a division.

One purpose of the simplified procedure of division was to encourage foreign groups, especially sugar people, to acquire land and begin business under the "Agricultural Concessions Law" of 1911. A concessionnaire was permitted to erect factories, build and maintain roads, railways, bridges and docks, improve ports and rivers, appropriate water for irrigation and construct the necessary works, including canals; to operate ships and tugs of foreign nationality, install telephones, telegraphs, wireless and electric plants, with the stipulation that electric current was not to be sold without executive permission. The produce was to be free from export tax for eight years, and the existing taxes could not be exceeded for twenty-five. Municipal taxes were limited to 2 percent ad valorem. Ships or convoys had to pay only half the regular port dues. Import duties on machinery for such enterprises were to be reduced 50 percent by discounting the stamped paper used for the purpose. All the concessionnaire had to do was to file the proper papers and buy or rent for ten years (in the case of sugar) the minimum amount of land (247.1 acres, or 100 *hectares*). Existing enterprises could come under the law by complying with its formalities.

To keep his franchise or concession, the grantee must begin work within a year, bring the minimum area under cultivation within two, and never abandon the concession for two consecutive years. No colonists excepting those of the white race could be brought in, but this provision was largely nullified by permissions to import harvest labor from neighboring islands and countries. One privilege was really extraordinary: where roads, railways, port improvements or other connecting works were found necessary, the state exercised its right of eminent domain in the interest of the foreigner by legally expropriating the required land. The 1910-11 Receivership Report (p. 23) characterized this law as "progressive," "framed along modern lines," and wise in its encouragement of the foreign capital so "absolutely necessary for the development of the country." It was certainly the "Magna Charta" of the foreign sugar industry!

This law was followed not only by a phenomenal expansion of sugar properties, but also by a harvest of typical "shoe-string" promotion schemes, which we need only mention. One of these was the Santo Domingo Planters Company, which proposed to enrich the stockholders it solicited by setting out 20,000 acres of raw land to cotton, on an initial capital of $100,000—which they were asked to furnish. Side by side with this interesting prospectus, issued in 1911 by Atwood Violett and Company, 20 Broad Street, New York City, the Pan-American Union's library at Washington has another, of *La Compañia Dominicana*, which is a fit companion for those of Cazneau and Fabens in an earlier period. "Uncle Sam," it stated, had guaranteed this "cradle of America," this "fair land of opportunity," against revolution for at least fifty years. "Santo Domingo," its writer asserted, "has a government as stable and on as high a plane as any government on earth—administered by some of the best and ablest men in America to-day. . . ." The ink was still wet on the prospectus when a new revolution broke out.

In setting up the 1907 Convention, the American Government had shut its eyes to the fact that it was dealing with a few able men in one political party. These had no idea of going out of office. A new constitution of 1908 had abolished the Vice-Presidency. Should the Presidency suddenly become vacant, the succession was left to an election by the Congress, which might be delayed for months and carried out under the shadow of military force. The ruling group calculated that its monopoly of the revenues through the American receivership removed all hope of successful opposition, and the Americans also frequently asserted that a serious revolution was impossible. A movement had started in 1909, only to be immediately crushed with American cooperation.

President Caceres, who was a strong man and a brave one, was riddled with bullets while taking a drive on Sunday afternoon, November 19, 1911. Velasquez had been regarded as his potential successor, but there was no guarantee of this. A temporary President was named by the Congress, pending an election. General Alfredo Victoria, who commanded the troops in the capital, forced the election of his uncle, the General himself being a mere youth, still under the constitutional age limit. After a farcical election, the elder Victoria became President of the Republic, February 27, 1912. Velasquez fled to Jamaica. Revolts had already broken out in various parts of the country, the most formidable led by Ex-President Horacio Vasquez, founder of Victoria's own political party. The Americans did nothing until the situation was entirely out of control. By the mere fact of running the customs receivership, they inevitably aided Victoria, who was both a usurper and incompetent. President Victoria's government was not only allowed to overdraw its legitimate funds in the hope of crushing a just revolution, but it was enabled by its official position to borrow or extort money on every hand, running up a formidable floating debt.

On January 31, 1912, just as the revolt was getting well under way, an American concern, led by two men named Jarvis and Niese, formally opened the *Banco Nacional de Santo Domingo*. It was a bank of emission, and hoped from the start to take the highly lucrative receivership account away from Michelena. President Francis J. R. Mitchell and his principals in New York were destined to play a great role in the rule of "deserving Democrats" under Secretary of State William Jennings Bryan. A three-cornered presidential campaign was on in the United States during 1912, greatly hampering any positive action in Santo Domingo. Late in March, Philander C. Knox, then Secretary of State, paid a visit to the Dominican capital. With him was William T. S. Doyle, who was to return later in the year to help settle Santo Domingo's two main troubles: the Haitian boundary dispute, and the revolution. In the midst of a revolution, Secretary Knox held up Santo Domingo as "a bright example to all the Americas and to the world, teaching the lesson that all free peoples are fit for good self-government. . . ." The revolt spread.

"Only complete control by our Government," wrote American Minister W. W. Russell, September 19,[7] "would permanently insure order and justice, but any degree of control would be beneficial; indeed, without our effective control, one administration here would be as good as another." This is the man who was to act with Doyle and General McIntyre in adjusting the trouble, and to be returned finally by the Wilson Administration after the notorious Sullivan had been recalled. Thus Russell is on record as wishing in 1912, under the Republicans, what he took part in consummating in 1916, under the Democrats. Something had to be done. The revolutionists took two custom-houses, besieged two others, and interfered with transport to inland cities.

The three Commissioners sent by the American Government forced President Victoria to resign by threats of withdrawing the customs revenues. A "good president"—that is, one approved by the Commissioners—would be granted American financial assistance in the form of a loan, "conditioned on approval of all disbursements by an auditor and financial advisor designated by the United States." The Dominican press raved about this invasion of the national independence, and wondered if the Wilson regime, on which they had set their hopes, would really be any improvement over those of the "irascible Rough Rider" and his less palatable successor, Taft. By this time, one of the mildest names for Roosevelt was the "modern Tartarin," and the Americans were "the goldfathers" (*los padrinos*). The "good president," *ad interim,* was Archbishop Nouel, a wonderful character and a man of great culture, but not a forceful administrator. His cloth was a handicap to him, as he was absolutely committed to general reconciliation. He made too many concessions, from which friction arose. Soon he grew despondent, his health began to fail, and he resigned after four months, instead of holding office for the two years planned. Thus in April, 1913, the newly installed Wilson Administration found an inextricable muddle on its hands, which Bryan, as Secretary of State, proceeded to complicate by the worst possible appointments.

One feature of this muddle which the Democrats inherited was the $1,500,000 loan promised to Archbishop Nouel's Government to cover the floating debt created by the revolution. There were three principal bidders: the Jarvis *Banco Nacional*, the Royal Bank of Canada, and the National City Bank of New York, represented in Santo Domingo by Santiago Michelena. When the award to the National City Bank was announced by the Bureau of Insular Affairs, Jarvis raised a fearful row in the Dominican press and protested to the State Department. He charged, and attempted to prove by figures in the public press, that his own bank's offer had been better, and strongly hinted that Doyle, of the Taft Commission, was also in the pay of the National City Bank. Bryan evidently suspected the truth of this. He turned Doyle out of the State Department and fell into the arms of the *Banco Nacional* crowd—steering himself onto one reef in his attempt to avoid another.[8] The spurious "greater and nobler Rome" speech, attributed to Elihu Root, had just swept through the press of Latin-America. It was an "impudent forgery," immediately denounced as such by its supposed author, but its allusions to the United States as the divinely appointed arbitrator of the destinies of all America were never overtaken by the repudiation.

CHAPTER VI

THE RULE OF DESERVING DEMOCRATS

> "Can you let me know what positions you have at your disposal with which to reward deserving Democrats? . . . You have had enough experience in politics to know how valuable workers are when the campaign is on and how difficult it is to find suitable rewards for all the deserving."
> WILLIAM JENNINGS BRYAN

JAMES MARK SULLIVAN was a deserving Democrat. Born in Ireland in 1873, he had arrived in America as a baby, achieved some education in the parochial schools of Massachusetts, and become a carpenter's apprentice at the age of sixteen. Turning to journalism, he had obtained a prize of one hundred dollars from the Hartford *Courant*, so the manager stated, by getting old subscribers to stop the paper and other members of the same families to take it instead. Later, as a prize-fight promotor, he was charged with appropriating the box-office receipts through a bogus attachment. Thus enabled to develop his talents in the Yale Law School during two years, he was sued by the tailor who made his graduation coat, won a valuable watch as a prize for oratory, but lost it, so he explained, in a "scuffle or fight in Waterbury." As a lawyer, he was never a member of any bar association. His most distinguished service to the profession consisted of inducing his friend "Bald Jack" Rose, the gambler, whom he had known since the famous getaway with the prize-fight funds, to "squeal" on Police Lieutenant Becker in the famous New York murder trial. He had known William C. Beer, Attorney for the *Banco Nacional de Santo Domingo,* since 1904, and Beer had thrown him odds and ends of law practice.

Sullivan's political work for the Democrats in the 1912 campaign put him in line for a good office. His application for the position of American Minister to Santo Domingo came naturally through his connection with Beer, attorney for the Jarvis bank. Bryan was well primed about the supposed wrong done the *Banco Nacional* by the award of the 1913 loan to the National City Bank. Various influential people connected with Beer, Jarvis or Mitchell, through the bank or otherwise, pressed the candidacy of Sullivan as the loyal, courageous man to see justice done. He was appointed August 12, 1913.[1]

Bryan's famous letter to Walker W. Vick, General Receiver of Dominican Customs, the most interesting passage of which is quoted at the head of this chapter, was dated August 20, 1913. It was printed in full in the *New York Times,* January 15, 1915, while Sullivan's conduct in office was under investigation. Secretary Bryan made the following comment, which appeared in the same paper the next day:

> "I am glad to have the public know that I appreciate the services of those who work in politics and feel an interest in seeing them rewarded. I think that is the only charge that can be based on that letter, and, as Mr. Vick received his appointment as a reward for political work, I thought he was a good man to address in expressing my opinion on the subject."

All this retort really established was that Mr. Vick, of New Jersey, was also a deserving Democrat, sent to Santo Domingo by President Wilson for the same reason that Bryan appointed James Mark Sullivan American Minister there. The belief of the Secretary of State that they would enjoy each other's society and work together in harmony was unfounded. Santo Domingo owes the shortness of their public careers partly to the zeal they displayed in collecting the large fund of stories about each other.

We may dismiss Mr. Vick's case with a very few words. The writer has gone through the Dominican newspaper files carefully, without finding any reference to the later charges of wastefulness and personal immorality up to the time of Vick's recall in 1914. Mr. Vick was not specially trained for his task by his previous career, but the Santo Domingo Chamber of Commerce publicly expressed regret at his going, in terms amounting almost to a protest. The author of the one most damaging letter used against him in the Sullivan investigation withdrew it when he found out that it was taken so seriously. If the Customs Receiver's personal standards of morality had been as charged—and that is as strong as any honest man can put it in the absence of proof—the Dominicans would not have been particularly shocked. This feature of the accusations did not impress them, even after it appeared. Santo Domingo is not New Jersey, or like it. It is highly unfortunate that the original Receiver, Mr. Pulliam, a specially trained and experienced man who (though nominally a Democrat) was satisfactory to the preceding Republican administrations and everybody else, had to be withdrawn by his own party for reasons which seem to us rather frivolous. They did to the Dominicans also.

Frederico Velasquez, father of the 1907 Convention, failed of election to succeed Archbishop Nouel as a temporary President. To break the deadlock between him and Ex-President Jimenez, a third man, José Bordas Valdez, was chosen. He was inaugurated April 14, 1913, for a term of one year, during which time an election was to be held. Picked largely for his amiable harmlessness, nobody seems to have suspected that he might stir up the momentarily dormant revolution by trying to seize power and succeed himself. His task might have dismayed a stronger man. The new National City Bank loan took an additional $30,000 a month out of the funds available to run the government. This meant a drop of 20 percent in utilizable income during the seven months following President Wilson's inauguration, as compared with the similar period in 1912. That is, the Democrats had inherited the Dominican problem at the very moment when it was fraught with the most difficulty and irritation. To make matters worse, this $1,500,000 loan arranged under the Taft administration lacked about $450,000 of covering the financial deficit. Hence, in spite of all the hardships demanded of the Dominican Government, it was doomed to see its debts mount, without being able to cover them.

A new revolt broke out in September, while Minister Sullivan was on his way to his post. The Bordas Government had sold a lease of the Dominican Central Railway to the highest bidder—to the only one, in fact. Governor Cespedes of the northern province of Puerto Plata, served by the road, protested that this meant bankruptcy, if it was not actually treason, and finally withdrew from the Bordas Government. Ex-President Horacio Vasquez (now—1927—President of the Re-

THE RULE OF DESERVING DEMOCRATS 57

public) was reported to be in the camp of the revolutionists. He was, in fact. It was now practically certain that Bordas meant to control the approaching election and succeed himself, which meant a herculean attempt to oust him by force. One leader saw this, and had the enterprise to take time by the forelock.

Secretary Bryan telegraphed Minister Sullivan, who was stopping off in Cuba on his way to Santo Domingo, authority to threaten the revolutionists with non-recognition if they should win, and to announce that the United States would not permit an increase of the public debt to meet their expenses or claims.[2] The force of the threat lay in the fact that the American customs receivership could withhold funds from an unrecognized government or refuse to advance them for buying off revolutionists. Sullivan knew nothing of statecraft, and had no idea of the consequences which sometimes follow simple-looking commitments. He promised the revolutionists immunity, payment of their expenses out of other than customs receipts, and "free and fair elections" if they would disarm, which they did. The vice of this scheme was that it committed the United States Government to something which it had no legal means of seeing honestly carried out. Sullivan insisted a little later that "President Wilson's declaration of principles concerning Latin America reserved the right to enter any Latin American country to see that the peoples' rights were not lost by force or fraud."[3]

What happened was that the State Department sent three representatives and twenty-nine agents to watch the Congressional election which took place at the beginning of December. A constitutional convention was to meet in January, 1914, and the President would be chosen later under whatever rules it adopted. Bordas reduced the "twenty-nine tourists," as the American agents were called in Santo Domingo, to mere observers. They were under the Chief Detective of the Porto Rican Police. Government forces broke up peaceful meetings of the opposition. Several lives were lost and a great deal of property destroyed in a riot in the capital which began in this way. Emiliano Tejera, one of the architects of the 1907 Convention, stated in a public letter that he would start impeachment proceedings against the President in the next Congress if a thorough investigation were not held. Force was employed at La Vega also, and the election was generally characterized as a farce, though Sullivan pronounced it satisfactory, thus committing the United States to the legality of the Congress it brought in.

The fat was in the fire. About a half million dollars of additional debt had been piled up by the September revolt. An election ridiculed in Santo Domingo but sponsored by the American Government had produced a Congress hostile to the President, many of its influential members being pledged to impeach him. Sullivan encouraged now one party, now another. He habitually used the public press for mixing in Dominican internal politics, a quotation from one of his published letters being used on one occasion to decorate a banner in front of party headquarters. In the end, he went back on the Congress provided by his own election, prevented a legal impeachment of Bordas, and even backed his candidacy for the presidency. No real business could be accomplished by the rival branches of the Government. President Bordas himself precipitated a new civil war by attacking General Arias. Sullivan encouraged the move, after consulting Secretary Bryan, and the American receivership made advances of money. By the end of

THE RULE OF DESERVING DEMOCRATS 59

May, 1914, the Government was in desperate military straits. Bryan almost exactly duplicated the move of the Republicans two years earlier. First issuing threats to "restore order," to make sure the Dominicans would take him seriously, he proposed the withdrawal of all the political leaders from the contest for the presidency, and that they should unite in support of "an honest and upright citizen of Santo Domingo who has no connection with politics or with the present situation"— in other words, another "good president" like Archbishop Nouel.

Two American Commissioners, Fort and Smith, set out from the United States at the beginning of August. As they left, a document summarizing what has been known as the "Wilson Plan" was handed to them. Incidently, a world war broke out while they were on their way to Santo Domingo. In brief, the "Wilson Plan"[4] called for the retirement of President Bordas, the appointment of a Provisional President, to be supported by the United States, and a new "free and fair election" of Congress and President, fully observed by American representatives. Minister Sullivan acted with the two Commissioners for a time, but he was so much in their way that one of them finally enticed him on a visit to the United States, leaving the other free to get some work done. Chargé White ran the legation for some months.

Bordas Valdez, whose term as President had long been up, was forced out of office, and a man named Baez acted as President until an election could be held in the fall (1914) under American supervision. Velasquez joined forces with Ex-President Jimenez, who was easily elected. Ex-President Vasquez was probably the strongest single candidate, but the coalition spoiled his campaign. Some of his followers refrained from voting, and the opposition of this political group was greatly feared. Secretary Bryan had long been for eliminating the troublesome General Arias. Ever since the General, then Governor at Monte Cristi, had been persuaded on an American warship in 1905 that his opposition to the receivership was futile, he had been a thorn in the side of the United States Government. Bryan proposed to get him out of the way with the aid of United States Marines, but President Baez demurred when asked to make the "request." Arias wielded a formidable political force, with which no Dominican politician was itching to start a fight. Previous ones had not turned out well. The newly elected President, Jimenez, was even less enthusiastic. Desiderio Arias had been one of his staunchest supporters in days when Jimenez was not so old and tired. He decided to buy the man off by making him Minister of War!

At last, the Wilson administration was pinned hard and fast to a situation which perfectly fitted the Latin-American program it had issued in the beginning. A temporary executive chosen under American supervision had decreed elections held under American observation. These elections had been accepted as fair and just, representing the "will of the people." The State Department was committed, specifically and in writing, to support the new government. No changes were to be tolerated except peaceful and constitutional ones. In setting up this new government, the Americans had themselves used methods unknown to the Dominican Constitution, ignored the existing legislative power, and employed threats of force against Arias. Their idea that the Congress and President they had sponsored would necessarily work together because both represented the "will of the people" rested on a nice and rather aged political fiction which did not correspond to anything in the realm of facts. It is one thing to get a mass of men who are in trouble, and do not know what they want, to act together once, quite another to hold them together after they have had a chance to elaborate an organization capable of expressing conflicting desires.

The "Wilson Plan" was fatally naïve at one point. Its creators did not see that President Jimenez, who in fact owed his office to the will of the American State Department as well as to that of the Dominican people, might have difficulty in carrying out the wishes of both. Acting-Secretary Lansing telegraphed Chargé White in December, 1914, to get a written pledge from Jimenez and Velasquez that they would "recognize position of Comptroller and . . . turn over to Receivership collection of internal revenues."[5] By the "Comptroller" was meant Charles M. Johnston, who had been appointed "financial expert," June 1, 1914, without the consent of the Dominican Congress. Here at last was the Financial Adviser, after the manner of the British in Egypt, if only the Dominicans could be induced to admit the legality of such an American officer under the 1907 Convention. Johnston had encountered endless difficulties and much open hostility. Chargé White secured a confidential letter from Jimenez and Velasquez, who did not dare make the required promise regarding American financial control publicly. The text of this letter has never been made public, but the men later claimed that they had not agreed to any control which could not be established constitutionally—that is, with the consent of Congress.

President Jimenez did what he could to reconcile the American demands with the entirely different wishes of the legislators, and split his government wide open in the process. Bryan also pressed for the abolition of the Dominican army and its replacement by a police force, organized with American aid. The Republican administration had made a similar suggestion in 1912. President Jimenez did not dare even mention this proposal to his Congress, and Sullivan counseled patience. Thus opened the year 1915, with Santo Domingo several millions of dollars behind, the American receivership still advancing $5,000 a day under State Department authorization, and nothing definitely settled. The Wilson Plan had elected two branches of a government, whereupon the Americans had tried to control one of these through the other and set them at loggerheads.

In February, 1915, the Dominican Congress twice voted down the proposed American financial control. Without it, the State Department would not sanction the loan necessary to fund the floating debt. The anomalous American comptroller served notice that after April 1, no payments would be made on certain budgetary items which he considered superfluous. This gage of battle the Congress took up immediately, passing a resolution to remove Johnston and rebuke Velasquez. There was even a good deal of talk and counting of probable votes for an impeachment of President Jimenez. Bryan had Sullivan "notify the plotters" that the United States would not tolerate this. The Dominican Congress declined to approve a credit order for $200,000 from the Public Works fund for use in building part of a road from the capital to La Vega, and the American State Department allowed the work to stop rather than go ahead without such sanction. President Jimenez's government was falling to pieces between the millstones of the Dominican Congress and the United States Government. He sent a delegation to Washington to ask for the withdrawal of the "financial expert" and also of a particularly irritating order of Bryan's which removed receivership appointments almost entirely from the supervision of Santo Domingo, whose revenues the people aided in collecting.

After a number of interviews with Secretary Bryan and President Wilson between May 6 and June 4, 1915, the American Department of State gave in on both points. A mistranslation of the letter announcing this fact led the Dominicans to maintain ever after that President Wilson had admitted the illegality of the appointment of a financial expert in withdrawing it. The State Department never went to the trouble to check up and clear up the misunderstanding, which was very careless on its part. The English version[8] stated that "the President of the United States has decided to avoid any question of the legality and propriety of the appointment of a financial expert for the Dominican Government or in the assignment of duties to such an expert which would in any way conflict with the Constitution or laws of the Dominican Republic," "which would in any way conflict" in the English version was translated into Spanish as "because they have conflicted" ("*porque resultaron uno y otros en conflicto*"). Franco-Franco did not have the English text, so he translated the Spanish (itself a translation) into French as *parce que cela était en conflit.*" Such is diplomacy. Each side repeatedly assumed the other's bad faith because of a childish error which either party could have discovered by replacing some of its belligerency with a little intelligent curiosity.

Bryan resigned as Secretary of State on June 9, 1915, five days after his final interview with the Dominican delegation. Robert Lansing held the post *ad interim* two weeks, and was then definitely appointed to it. He understood the traditions of the State Department, but made the terrible mistake of thinking he could go back to them at once, disregarding the mountain of blunders left behind by the deserving Democrats of the Bryan period. Able in his own way, Lansing nevertheless lacked the imagination of the best men who have served us in the post. Johnston, whatever his technical capacities, was unacceptable in Santo Domingo. Lansing merely moved him to the "Statistical Department" of the Receivership. This was interpreted by the Dominicans as evasion and bad faith. President Jimenez telegraphed President Wilson that Charles Johnston was unacceptable in any capacity, but Lansing stood his ground, and the dispute grew more bitter than ever. Minister Sullivan finally cleared out at the close of the Bryan regime. Chargé Stewart Johnson ran the Legation until October 3, 1915, when William W. Russell, ancient apostle of "control," arrived to resume the duties of Minister.

Sullivan and Bryan had completely undermined American prestige. To many Dominicans, Uncle Sam was a wolf looking for a lamb to devour, and to most of the rest he was an ass whose capricious heels had to be watched. The unliquidated debt had been estimated by the American "financial expert" at around $7,000,-000. This guess was several millions too high, but the situation was absolutely hopeless and the figure does not greatly matter. Each side blamed the other, and the deficit went on mounting. The Public Works fund, which still contained over $3,000,000, was tied up by the quarrel between President Jimenez and his Congress, the American Government siding with the former. The

Jarvis-Mitchell *Banco Nacional* had advanced a good deal of money to the Dominican Government, on Minister Sullivan's recommendations. He had gotten the receivership account transferred to this bank late in 1913, but the concern was too weak to handle it, and Michelena got it back in a few months. Sullivan used the bank for a downtown office, and its personnel for interpreters. He persistently overdrew his account, and had to be rebuked by the State Department. His cousin, Timothy Sullivan, who had no technical capacity, was mixed up in Public Works contracts. A Jarvis subsidiary was made purchasing agent in New York. The bank combination was all the more suspicious because the Minister of Foreign Relations of Santo Domingo was the uncle of one of Jarvis's associates.

There were doubts as to the legality of the *Banco Nacional's* advances to the Dominican Government. Several hundred thousands of dollars were involved in the question, which the State Department sent a special counsel down to investigate. Sullivan approached this man and offered to find him more lucrative employment as the bank president's attorney at the close of the job! As Commissioner Phelan stated in his report at the close of investigation of the Minister's conduct:

> "I am not satisfied beyond a reasonable doubt that Mr. Sullivan fully realized the grossness of the impropriety of his proposition, but I am satisfied because of his proposition that he is not a proper person to hold the position that he does hold."

Sullivan's usefulness in Santo Domingo was finally and completely destroyed by the publication of a letter he had written concerning the "savage, brutal tendencies of a semi-civilization," in which "the men of this generation are hopeless, the highest aspiration of the best being to make public office the means for private plunder." Four Dominican editors clubbed together to write an open letter to the Minister of Foreign Affairs, demanding the Minister's recall. Even "the grafting tactics manifested by him under cover of his diplomatic position" did not constitute the main grievance. "It is," they wrote, "that we do not consent that Mr. James Mark Sullivan continue to insult us, either with his letters and his insolent meddling or with his odious presence."

CHAPTER VII

FROM THREATS TO FORCE

It is a wonderful Government for doing the things it does not intend to do, and the very things it would not do if it knew that it was doing them.—GEORGE BERNARD SHAW.

HAITI and Santo Domingo were both nominally republics in 1914-15. They occupied the two ends of the same island. Each had suffered too many revolutions for its own good. The Haitian population is black, much denser than that of Santo Domingo, and the masses speak a dialect which is a corruption of Old French, though a modern Frenchman has to learn it, just as he does Spanish or Italian. Once learned, it is extremely crude and inadequate. The *"Nègre"* or *"Neg"* of Louisiana, spoken by and to the slaves in the old days, was quite similar, and was never confused with the actual French used by the master class in addressing each other.

Like parts of Cuba, especially some years ago, Haiti still has astonishing vestiges of African voodooism which neither the law nor the French priests have been able to break up. This is not the place to describe the savage superstitions or their occasional tragic results with which the writer has come into personal contact, and he doubts if the naked truth would be believed. Very good Spanish is spoken in Santo Domingo, with somewhat of an accent, and there is nothing to startle a Southern European in the Roman Catholic religion which obtains there. The cases of Haiti and Santo Domingo in 1914-15 were very different, but the American State Department mistook a surface resemblance for real similarity and sought to apply the same program. A Haitian revolution of October, 1914, led to the landing of American Marines, followed by a presentation, word for word, of the "Wilson Plan" then being tried in Santo Domingo. Haiti was pressed to accept an American customs receivership modeled on that of Santo Domingo, with the Financial Expert carefully inserted in the text to avoid possible argument later.

The systematic Marine occupation of Haiti began at the end of July, 1915, following a riot in which the President was assassinated. This was during a momentary lull in the American dispute with Santo Domingo over financial control, just at the beginning of the Lansing regime in our State Department. American Naval and Marine Corps officers interfered in various ways with Haitian politics, obtained a President satisfactory to them, and assumed practical oversight of the Government beginning with September, 1915. The *Listin Diario* of Santo Domingo remarked in an editorial entitled "The Godfathers," August 9: "The fire is getting close, and any spark may set off our powder." How the American officers in Haiti forced through a treaty establishing a protectorate, called all who opposed them *cacos* or bandits and made good their authority over those who remained alive, concerns us here only as it affects the Dominican situation. Events in Haiti between July and December, 1915, silenced most of the defenders of American policy in Santo Domingo. Just as the Americans had believed that they could impose customs supervision in Haiti because they had done so in Santo Domingo, it seemed to them after September, 1915, that they should be able to establish a more general control over Santo Domingo, as they had done in Haiti.

Acting Secretary of State Polk handed Minister Russell a letter of instructions, dated September 17,[1] which was nothing more or less than an outline of the scheme then being imposed upon Haiti. This date is the day following the signing of the treaty by the Haitian Government. Minister Russell arrived in Santo Domingo in the early days of October. He was to inform the Government there that the United States claimed the right, under the 1907 Convention, to appoint a financial adviser and to enlarge the Customs Guard or create a constabulary. Minister Russell prepared his note, later famous all over Latin-America as "Russell's No. 14," dated November 19, 1915, from these instructions signed by Polk. The wording is in many places identical.[2]

This note alluded so clumsily to alleged improprieties on the part of the government addressed that the text could not be given to the press. What the newspapers did was to print the actual demands in their nakedness, without any of the logical and historical wrappings in which they had been done up by the American Minister. The proposals were, in brief: (1) A financial adviser, plus control of all collections and expenditures, including those not mentioned in the 1907 Convention; (2) Complete suppression of the Army and Republican Guard, and the creation of a constabulary with American officers; (3) Reduction of the national budget, and revision of revenues. The manner of making the demands could not have been more maladroit. President Jimenez, almost the only friend the Americans had, could not publish the note, as it would throw his administration wide open to attacks by its enemies. When he withheld it, he was accused on the floor of the Chamber of Deputies of secret negotiations with the Americans. By April, 1916, the Cabinet had begun to break up. The President's son had taken charge of the Ministry of Finance. Arias, Minister of War, and Jacinto Peynado, Minister of the Interior, were political enemies, plotting for each other's scalps. Hardly anyone in the parliamentary minority which still worked more or less with President Jimenez was willing to follow him very far in concessions to the United States.

Suspecting that a coup was being prepared against him, the President practically kidnapped the commander of the fortress in the capital, and also the head of the Republican Guard. This unconstitutional act aroused the fears of all the opposition in Congress. Put together, they made up a good sized majority. The Minister of War surmised, not unnaturally, that the arrest of his subordinates without consulting him was merely the beginning of a coup d'état, and that his turn would come next. He occupied the fortress himself, declaring that the move was in the interest of a peace which the President's act had disturbed, and explicitly disavowing the intention of attacking anybody. Velasquez understood the attitude of the Americans toward Minister Arias personally, and remained neutral. The other leaders sided with Arias in his dispute with the President, against whom regular impeachment proceedings were initiated in the Congress. This was May 1. Instead of awaiting the result, the President, who was at his country place, marched on the capital with an improvised army. American troops were landed the morning of the 4th, ostensibly to protect the Legation. By the 6th, it was evident that President Jimenez would not be able to take the capital. Minister Russell and Admiral Caperton (who had arrived from Haiti) offered him enough Americans for the job. He accepted at first, but immediately withdrew the request, choosing to resign his office rather than march against a regularly elected Congress behind foreign bayonets.[3]

All that now remained of the product of the Wilson-Plan election was the Congress. Under the Dominican Constitution, the Ministers were appointees of the President, to aid him in the transaction of administrative business. In case his office became vacant, the Constitution gave them only one function: that of convoking Congress if it were not in session, so that it could name an ad interim President until a regular one could be elected. Congress being in session, the Cabinet had no further duties whatever. Article 32 of the Constitution definitely assigned all residual powers, not specifically attributed to any other organ of the State, to the Congress. Despite the irregularity involved in presenting it direct to the people, the President's resignation evidently created a vacancy in the office.

Force, not legality, settled the issue of the executive power. The American force, exercised under Minister Russell and Admiral Caperton, was obviously superior. These men were determined not to let the Congress choose a President, for fear one hostile to them would be elected. They hit upon the fiction of considering the four remaining Jimenez Ministers as "continuers of the executive power." The mystery of why these Ministers did not resign, instead of allowing themselves to be thrust into a ridiculous and unconstitutional position, was finally cleared up by one of them, Jimenez's son, in testifying before the American Senate Investigating Committee in 1921:[4]

> ... "I wish to state that the secretaries of state and I, above all, whose mission had ended, wanted to resign also, but Minister Russell told us that we ought not to do so, because the country would be without a government, and it would be necessary to appoint an American military governor. For that reason we continued in office."

Their attempt to save their country from the carrying out of this threat proved futile in the end.

Admiral Caperton could fancy as many "revolutionaries" and "bandits" in Santo Domingo as he had "*cacos*" in Haiti. He appears to have believed he could eliminate General Arias and Ex-President Vasquez as easily as he had the leading candidate for the Haitian Presidency, Dr. Bobo; use Federico Velasquez as neatly as he had Dartiguenave; and get rid of the Dominican Congress as readily as the Haitian. Minister Russell stood at his elbow, asking for a whole regiment of Marines where the Admiral would have been content with five hundred. Secretary Lansing lent his "approval" or "concurrence" from time to time, and let this pair try their hands at the game of statecraft, aided by overwhelming force and dealing with constitutional restrictions merely as inconvenient obstacles.

Congress met May 11, and proceeded to consider, not General Arias, but Ramón Báez, who had served as temporary President under the Wilson Plan, and Federico Henriquez y Carvajal, Chief Justice of the Supreme Court. Neither was in any sense a partisan politician. Admiral Caperton delivered an ultimatum to General

FROM THREATS TO FORCE

Arias on May 13 to disarm the Dominican forces and turn over the material to the Americans by 6 A. M. of the 15th, and warned the city of the bombardment which would take place if resistance were offered.[5] During the night of May 14, the Dominican forces marched off, taking all the arms and ammunition they could carry and also enlisting the prisoners who had been held in the fortress. Santo Domingo would have been saved years of guerilla warfare and much outright banditry if the Admiral had shown a little more decision and actually disarmed these people instead of merely chasing them to the hills with a threat. Since both courses were equally arbitrary and unconstitutional, there was no excuse for not following the more practical one. It is particularly dangerous to be arbitrary and weak-willed at the same time.

When Minister Russell found out that the birds had flown, he called for immediate occupation, and the Marines took over the capital. In publishing the Russell-Caperton threat, the Mayor had stated that the American Minister had given assurances that the object of landing American troops was "to guarantee the free election by the Chambers of the new President of the Republic." Nevertheless, Russell asked the Presidents of the Chambers "not to meet for two or three days, until the city recovers its normal aspect."[6] The name of Judge Henriquez y Carvajal had already passed two of the three required readings in the Deputies, which reassembled on the 17th and elected him, subject to three votes in the Senate. The same day that Minister Russell told the Dominicans to wait "two or three days," he wrote Secretary Lansing that in his "opinion Congress should not be allowed to proceed with election President until peace restored in entire Republic." He proposed to keep obstructing and putting off the election until he could get rid of the candidates he did not want. There is no use in calling this anything but plain duplicity.

Lansing made the suggestion that the legality of President Jimenez's resignation might be questioned! Four Senators were clapped into prison during the night of June 4-5, to prevent the name of Judge Henriquez y Carvajal from passing the third reading the next day, which would have elected him temporary President. The Judge withdrew his candidacy under American pressure. Just at this juncture, Marines were landed on the northern coast, Puerto Plata was taken by storm, and the Americans marched from Monte Cristi to the most important inland city, Santiago, which capitulated. Even after the general occupation had been decided upon, Russell continued to juggle for a President of his choice and the protectorate demanded in his Note No. 14 of the previous November. He had only until July 27 to get his President with any semblance of legality, as the mandate of Congress expired on that date. He would not accept either Vasquez or Arias, and the only other candidate he took seriously was Federico Velasquez. Velasquez was to be the goat—playing the role of President Dartiguenave in Haiti. But Velasquez was not a Dartiguenave. When he heard of a scheme to make him *de facto* President, he eliminated himself by a correct but very firm telegram to the Governor of Puerto Plata.[7]

In the meantime (June 18), Minister Russell had notified the rump "Council" of four, executive by grace of an American interpretation of the Dominican Constitution, that the American receivership was that day assuming the collection of all the revenues of Santo Domingo, and would henceforth act also as paying agency.[8] Minister Jimenez immediately resigned. The three remaining "continuers of the executive power" were all under suspicion at the American Legation, as they had protested against the seizure as illegal.

Congress surprised everybody by unanimously electing Francisco Henriquez y Carvajal as Provisional President July 25—two days before the end of the session. He was a brother of the Supreme Court Judge, and had himself been a Judge in the Permanent Court of Arbitration at The Hague, besides holding other distinguished positions in international bodies. For many years he had been living in Cuba, and had no connection with current Dominican politics. His negotiations in connection with the debt situation fifteen years earlier have been mentioned in a previous chapter.

President Henriquez y Carvajal picked a non-political cabinet of the most distinguished brains in the country. Only Cabral y Baez, who took charge of Foreign Relations, had been a Cabinet Minister before. Francisco J. Peynado, a lawyer of international reputation, was made Minister of Finance. He had been Minister to Washington, had made over thirty visits to the United States, and was known as an admirer of American institutions. Arias was no longer an issue. He had disbanded the army and quietly settled down to private life. The Americans now had a Dominican Government to deal with, and over it they held a tremendous club: They could refuse it recognition and hold up its funds until it signed up for the Haitian-type protectorate outlined in Russell's No. 14. The following "important notice" appeared in the daily newspapers:

IMPORTANT NOTICE

Santo Domingo, August 18, 1916.

In accordance with instructions from Washington, and supplementary notice transmitted through the American Minister in Santo Domingo, the receiver general will not deliver any more funds on the Government's account under the control of the public treasury of Santo Domingo, established on the 16th of June, 1916.

This suspension of payment will continue until some complete understanding regarding the interpretation of certain articles of the American-Dominican convention of 1907 be arrived at, interpretation of which the Government of the United States has insisted on and of which the Dominican Government has knowledge since the month of November last, or until the present Dominican Government has been recognized by the Government of the United States.

C. H. BAXTER, Receiver General.

"Since the month of November last" referred to Russell's Note No. 14, which President Henriquez y Carvajal had never seen. It was now published in installments in the daily press (August 22-24). The storm it raised in Santo Domingo can be imagined. Assured that all the invaders wanted was a "free election," Dominicans generally had opposed almost no resistance at the outset, and very little even in June and July, when the more general occupation had taken place. Now it was clear that this meant the "free election" of a President satisfactory to the American Minister, and that Henriquez y Carvajal would fill the bill only if he decided to underwrite the Note No. 14 protectorate. It was too late to resist by force, as the Marines were already in possession. Four years later, Fabio Fiallo, statesman, poet and editor, was to get into trouble for stating that the Marines had arrived "through the back door with fixed bayonets in a dark night of deceit." Making due allowance for the Spanish way of putting things, this was not an unnatural way for a Dominican to look at the process described above. An American military court was to find it worthy of a heavy fine and a long prison sentence.

President Henriquez y Carvajal was obliged to accept the American seizure of financial control, as he admitted. It was an accomplished fact. He also admitted the necessity of conceding the point of an American-officered police force to replace the Dominican army, the latter being already practically disbanded and the Marines left in control. Minister Russell wanted all this done by a decree, but the President declined to sign one, on the ground that he had no constitutional right to do so. To his mind, the fact that the Dominican Government agreed to take care of the changes ought to be sufficient, especially as the Americans already had possession of the force and the revenues. Russell would not give an inch. Greatly to the surprise of the Americans, the Dominican Government kept on month after month, in spite of their appropriation of its funds. Instead of weakening, the attitude of the country stiffened as one fatal incident after another occurred under Marine control. At last, the Americans grew uncomfortably aware that they were getting the blame for the gradual disintegration of economic life, as well as for the growth of banditry. They were too few to keep order, and the Dominican forces which might have done so had been scattered, either deliberately or as a result of the stoppage of funds to pay them. Dominicans generally were merely contemptuous of the charge that their Government was the one responsible, because it had refused to accept the protectorate. To avoid the responsibility involved, and also to forestall the election of a new Congress (which would have been at least as hostile as the old) the American Military Government was proclaimed at the end of November.[9]

A few incidents which occurred in the intervening months will serve to illustrate some of the inevitable features of foreign military control. A momentary chance for reconciliation offered itself at the end of August, when the six-million-dollar American cruiser *Memphis* was piled up on the reef at Santo Domingo City in a hurricane, with a loss of thirty lives and the ship. Her cost alone was more than the whole amount at which the Dominican floating debt was finally bonded. That more of her crew of seven hundred were not lost was due in part to the heroic efforts of the civilian population, and a lively sympathy manifested itself for the time being. Nothing was made of it, as the Dominican Government would not take the unconstitutional step of decreeing the full protectorate without the action of Congress, and the Americans would not accept less. A notice which appeared in the daily papers of Sepember 14 marked a definite turning point. It was signed by "H. I. Bears, Major, U. S. M. C." All permits to carry arms dated before August 12 were revoked. Unfortunately, this move was more or less successful, and the defenseless population was terrorized by bandits. Moreover, the carrying out of the order led to the most exasperating incidents.

Major Bears stormed at the press, which insisted upon publishing unsympathetic accounts of the forcible entries of Marines into Dominican homes in search of arms. He called upon the Provincial Governor to stop the "attacks," only to be reminded by that official that such a move was not among his legal functions, speech and printing being free under the Constitution. If abuses occurred, there were the courts! According to Governor Sanchez's report of this interview, published in the daily papers September 19, the Major shouted at this juncture that "the laws have never been obeyed in this country!" The Governor stated that he was not going to be coerced by the Americans into breaking the fundamental law of the country, but added that the situation looked grave, and the editors had better "reflect with due maturity." A press association was organized two days later. Four of its original council of six were to feel the iron hand of military vengeance in due time. The worst feature of this organization, from the American point of view, was that no censorship could be made severe enough to entirely prevent the leakage of news to other Latin-American countries. In spite of the fines and imprisonment later resorted to, the press as a whole made it a point of honor to keep as near the dead-line as possible. Often enough, an editor's foot slipped, his paper was suspended, and he was himself prosecuted. The limits of what would be tolerated were hard to set before the proclamation of a Military Government made a formal censorship possible by creating the fiction of a reign of "law" which the foreigners could control for their own purposes. Some papers were suspended even before this period; but as a general thing, the editors continued to publish the news with any comments they saw fit to make. We may note some of the items.

A cabman named José Augusto was killed for "trying to get away" on November 5. He had tried to tell a group of Marines who were beating up one Pedro Cabrera that the man (who could not explain himself, as he spoke only the national language) had nothing to do with the matter for which he was being beaten. A sergeant forced the cabman at the point of a pistol to break the law by driving him through the historic "27th of February" gate, and also threatened a city policeman with the weapon when the latter expostulated. During the evening of November 14, a group of Marines forced themselves into the house of a woman whose name, street and number were given in the press accounts. They made themselves comfortable for a time, and then proceeded to throw furniture and utensils out into the street. In leaving, they pounded on nearby doors, and in the general row managed to run down and hurt a little girl. On another occasion, a small boy who was driving some sheep down a side street was beaten because Marines suspected him, groundlessly as the passersby stated, of having thrown stones at them.

Aside from the killings, of which there were a good many, most of the incidents seem trivial enough, and often had more than one side. For example, the cabman Augusto was armed, like most of the others who drove at night, and Dominican permits were not recognized by the Marines. He made a break for liberty after being disarmed, and was shot down as he ran. This clearly raised the issue of the legality of Marine control. To a Dominican, who denied the implied legal right, the act was murder; to the Marines it was a policing incident. In Latin countries, even a policeman is not supposed to shoot a man known to be disarmed. The sergeant mentioned above may not have known that one does not pass through the "27th of February" gate, any more than he uses the flag for a carpet. Señora X———, whose furnishings were tossed about with such joyful abandon, did not live on a particularly nice street, and the papers refrained from mentioning her source of livelihood. Such a case of drunkenness and disorderly conduct was difficult for the Americans to explain. The wounding of the child was of course accidental. A grown person is always in the wrong in beating up a passing boy, but such things do happen occasionally, even in perfectly orderly countries. There are always several kinds of people, all more or less human, in a group like the Marine Corps. The idea here is not to whitewash any of them who may have done wrong, but to bring into relief the more important fact that it was their presence as a foreign military force, not their identity, that made the trouble. Perhaps the best illustration of this is the Duarte riot at the end of October, 1916.

Villa Duarte is a suburb across the Ozama River, opposite the capital. The wagon bridge which now exists was not yet finished in 1916, and boats were used to reach this wooded region. General Ramon Batista, who was wanted by the Americans for an attack on a revenue cutter the previous year, was reported to be at a house in Villa Duarte. Note that the crime for which it was desired to try him belonged to the period before the military occupation. Captain Lowe, Lieutenant Morrison, two sergeants, three soldiers and an interpreter crossed the river October 24 to get the General. How hard they tried to take him alive is not clear, as the party was thrown into disorder and very nearly cleaned out by the friends and relatives of Batista after he had been shot.

This was only the beginning. Reinforcements were sent across the river with machine guns. Among the non-combatants hit in the mêlée were two women, one of whom died later of a wound in the abdomen. The Marines were naturally nervous that day, after their casualties. One Manual Diaz, a musician, was shot in another quarter of the city, dying the next morning. A patrol returning from Villa Duarte the evening of the 28th stopped to question Felix M. Cueves, proprietor of the cafe "Polo Norte," who was just closing up his place for the day. He was sixty-one years old, deaf, and did not understand English, even when shouted at him. The Marines later claimed that a shot was fired at them. They riddled Cueves with bullets and bayonets practically at arm's length, killed a man named Ruiz who came to the door to see what was going on, and proceeded to shoot up the neighborhood. One ball killed a boy who was eating his dinner in one of the thin-walled houses nearby, and another wounded a servant girl.

Everything which happened in the chain of fatal events became probable the moment a detachment of foreign soldiers was sent out to settle a pre-occupation score. As some readers of these lines will know from experience, it is trying to be freely shot at from ambush, and almost as trying to expect it. Military law is intentionally and necessarily frightful. Those who send in the soldiers, not the men themselves, are responsible for what occurs afterward. A properly drilled body of troops being the most mechanized of human groups, its probable conduct is the easiest of all to predict. The Americans were well aware of what they were doing when the first landing was made in Santo Domingo. Minister Jimenez reported an interview with the officer concerned, Captain Crossley, as follows:[10]

"But as on effecting the landing of the forces some shots might be fired, he pointed out that martial law would immediately be put in force, and as the military law is very severe, if the place from which the shot was fired could not be ascertained, the marines would have to fire at every living being —women, children, or aged persons. Those are the exact words of Capt. Crossley."

The Captain was performing both his duty and an act of kindness in explaining just what happens under military occupations, whether they are in Santo Domingo, in Eastern France and Belgium, or elsewhere. Assuming that General Batista personally got exactly what he deserved, there is still some question as to whether the American nation could afford to have justice carried out in its name in just this fashion, and with all these incidental trimmings.

Military Government resting purely on force, and there being no fiction about the popular derivation of this force, the application must be ruthless and overwhelming if slips are not to occur. Let us add "often," as some accidents will happen anyhow. Clerk Brewer, left in charge of the American Legation while Minister Russell was in Washington arguing for a military government, thought the death of Captain Low in the Duarte riot "probably due to absence of impressive force." A dispatch from Secretary Lansing in the 1916 volume of *Foreign Relations* shows that he was willing to put all Santo Domingo formally under martial law as early as October 28. It is necessary to distinguish between the military *occupation*, which took place more or less gradually after the landing early in May, and the military *government*, which was not proclaimed till the end of November. The second and more drastic step was taken because the first had failed, producing the drawbacks of military rule without its fruits. It was believed that the final and complete resort to force would bring the Dominicans to terms. This is evident from the early correspondence of the American Military Governor. He complained that the rump executive council had "deserted," leaving no constitutional power from which a legal protectorate could be exacted. There was nothing to do but supply American "cabinet officers." Captain Knapp later congratulated himself[11] that chance had enabled him to go ahead without Dominican cooperation. It made the difference between a protectorate, which rests upon an agreement between two governments, and a rule of force, founded solely upon the will of one.

What else could the Americans have done in the Fall of 1916, other than to set up a military dictatorship? Probably the one alternative at that late date was to accept the Dominican Government's offer of financial and police control. Under the "deserving Democrats," the floating debt had been allowed to pile up to heights which would have been impossible in the presence of any consistent policy. Creditors had much reason to suppose that unfunded debts would be covered later, as the Bryan-Sullivan regime repeatedly permitted them to be contracted, its protegé, the *Banco Nacional*, being one of the big lenders. That is, the United States was not wholly free from responsibility. A Dominican Government under American supervision might have installed steel filing cabinets and the latest accounting methods less rapidly than did the alien military force. Legitimacy is worth something, however, even at a sacrifice of mechanical efficiency. There would have been less doubt as to whether those who resisted a legally constituted government of Dominicans were bandits, or merely patriots—less occasion to compare American with Prussian rule, to the disadvantage of the former. This is not a theoretical case, as the comparison was often made in Santo Domingo.

CHAPTER VIII

SETTING UP A MILITARY DICTATORSHIP

Where troops have been quartered, brambles and thorns spring up.—LAO TZU

CAPTAIN H. S. KNAPP, Commander of the Cruiser *Force*, United States Atlantic Fleet, issued the "Proclamation of Occupation" from the Flagship *Olympia*, November 29, 1916. It appeared in the daily papers the next day, and was printed December 2 in the *Gaceta Oficial* in both Spanish and English. At the close of the Spanish version was inserted a sentence which left no doubt as to who was in control, or what language he spoke: *"El texto original de esta Proclamación, en el idioma inglés, regirá en toda cuestión de interpretación."* The *English* original ruled in all questions of interpretation, and the American Military Government would not even assume the responsibility for its own translation into the language of the country. This is not an isolated or unfair illustration of the point it carries. Repeatedly, military courts held Spanish-speaking natives to the American version of the English text of the Executive Orders which passed for laws. It was no excuse that the accused could not read English, or that the translation into Spanish under the direction of the Military Government said something different. The implied assumption that the native was the better educated of the two was never used to his advantage.

SETTING UP A MILITARY DICTATORSHIP   87

Alleged violations of Article III of the 1907 Convention and disturbances of domestic tranquillity such as to threaten "future observance" were the excuses named. Dominican laws were to be "recognized" only in so far as they did not conflict with the objects or regulations of the foreign military. These laws might even be administered by Dominicans, if the Americans thought this necessary, "all under the oversight and control of the United States forces." A censorship was proclaimed at the same time, covering publicity of every kind. The preliminary announcement that no one could have arms or explosives without American permission was followed by a detailed notice, dated December 5, emanating from the "Office of the Provost Marshal" and signed by Captain Walter N. Hill. It canceled all permits antedating the Marine seizure of power and decreed that they must be turned in at the designated American officer's bureau with the accompanying arms. The one piece of cheerful news was that the Americans meant to resume budget payments out of the funds they had been withholding since August 18. Having thus "brought an economic crisis in the country," as the State Department had aptly put it, the time was now at hand to take the credit for curing it.

Executive Order No. 12 informed the public without any waste of words: "For the present, and until further notice, no elections will be held in the Republic of Santo Domingo."[1] Exit the hope of a new Congress. Executive Order No. 18[2] cleaned up the last vestiges of constitutional government by suspending the existing Congress, on the ground that there was no quorum anyhow. Of course one could not be supplied without an election, which had already been forbidden. Captain Knapp decided that the executive branch had eliminated itself.

He had waited for some days, and its members had not come forward with offers to cooperate. To be exact, Executive Order No. 4, which appeared in the *Gaceta Oficial,* December 13, declared that these ministers "having failed . . . to administer or attempt to administer their offices under the Military Government as patriotic Dominicans acting in the interest of the country, are declared removed from office and their offices are declared vacated." The names of the American successors of these "unpatriotic" gentlemen followed.

Force, if adequate, greatly simplifies things. It was awkward not to have cabinet officers. For example, there was still over $3,000,000 of Dominican money in the Public Works Fund, derived from the 1905-7 collections and the 1908 loan. To build roads with this money and make a showing, there had to be somebody with at least the fiction of authority to sign the orders. An American officer, as "Minister of Finance," would answer. This might be illegal, but that could be cured later by making the Dominicans legalize it as part of the price of handing them back their country. According to the Receivership Report for 1916,[3] the total collections from August to December, inclusive, amounted to $1,713,308.91. Some of this was collected before August 18, and some belonged to the foreign creditors, but there was a tidy sum of more than a half million dollars left over.

The Military Government always insisted that it found the Dominican Treasury empty and fourteen thousand dollars in debt.[4] Why not? Funds had been held back for months, while hundreds of thousands of dollars accumulated. Lieutenant Commander Mayo's pronouncements on this subject are a little taxing to our credulity. Obviously the Military Government did not

SETTING UP A MILITARY DICTATORSHIP 89

suddenly get the money to resume budget payments out of a magician's hat. The long poverty of the Henriquez y Carvajal Government is the other side of the sudden wealth of the new Dictators. Besides this ready money to start operations with, there was the big Public Works Fund to invest in the more distant aspects of making a showing, such as roads. These sums were already in existence, and belonged to Santo Domingo. One of the first moves was to get even with the lenders who had helped to make it possible for the Dominican Government to hold out for months. Salaries were paid only to employees personally. They could then do as they liked about cheating their creditors, who had enabled them to live while the foreigners were holding back the pay which really belonged to them. That some of these creditors were usurers was the excuse for striking at them as a class. It has probably never occurred to most Americans that their taxes covered a good sized salary account in Santo Domingo, where most of the high officers and many other people drew United States Navy pay. Finally, the European war had been going on more than two years, and the prices of Santo Domingo's characteristic products were entering the greatest boom in their history. If ever a governing group had a chance to make a showing, it was the American Military Government of Santo Domingo.

A "patriotic Dominican," as the people who now had the force defined him, was a man who rushed forward to help make the Military Government a success. Governor Perez, of Pacificador Province, did not feel this way. He even marched a small force against the Americans. Lest anybody should mistake his sentiments for patriotism, Executive Order No. 3 made the following declaration:

"Lico Perez, until recently Civil Governor of Pacificador province, having revolted and engaged in acts of hostility against the Occupation, is hereby declared an outlaw, and the office that he had is declared vacant."[5]

Executive Order No. 20 removed the Dominican Minister to the United States who had followed instructions in presenting a protest against the seizure of his country. Similarly, the Dominican Chargé d'Affaires at Havana was fired for signing a protest which, the Americans charged, "contained inflammatory and false statements." The Minister who discharged this disloyal public servant, Señor Morillo, bore the good old Dominican name of Chandler, signing himself "L. H. Chandler, Captain, U. S. N.[6]

The International Banking Corporation of New York City, subsidiary of the National City Bank, now deemed Santo Domingo safe for a branch. Jarvis had shown poor technique in fighting Michelena by starting the rival *Banco Nacional*. The National City group simply bought out Michelena, having ascertained that the position of depositary of receivership funds would be included in the bargain. Executive Order No. 42, dated March 20, 1917, announced the change as taking effect April 1.

Having laid its hands on the central machinery of government, the Military Government now turned to the communes. So that the councils would remain in office, without elections and thus in spite of the Constitution, it was simply "ordered" that their corporate life should continue, and should be held to have continued. Lest they should mistake a convenient toleration for something more, the order[7] finally stated: "The continu-

SETTING UP A MILITARY DICTATORSHIP 91

ance in office of the present personnel of the Ayuntamientos is at the pleasure of the Military Government. Unless and until otherwise ordered, such personnel is continued."

No government in our time goes so far as to admit that it is not even *"for* the people." Captain Knapp's proclamation had destroyed the useful slogan of "government *by* the people." As Rear-Admiral Robison stated the problem later:[8] "Some working doctrine was essential upon which to base our conduct of affairs. It was found in the thought that the military Government administers the government of the Dominican Republic in trust for the Dominican people, in whom, in the words of Article 13 of the Dominican constitution, 'sovereignty is vested solely.'" Thus the Military Government based its rule on a thought—one of its own. "Government" and "constitution" began with small letters when they were modified by "Dominican," but "Government" was capitalized when it was American and military. I refer to the actual text.

Rear-Admiral Robison's "working doctrine" had at least the merit of recognizing the facts. The United States had taken possession of a weaker country by force, and had ample force to hold it. A "working doctrine," to translate the only will that counted into action, was all the theory the Military Governors needed. Their meaning is nearly always clear, because it expressed merely action, past or to come. It is some comfort to understand, even when we cannot quite agree. When we turn to the thousands of pages of more theoretical argument as to whether the occupation was "legal" or "justified," we are not always so fortunate.

Perdomo, the Dominican Minister at Washington, immediately enumerated the main reasons why his Government regarded the setting up of the Military Government by force as a violation of international law and of the principles of Pan-Americanism. Later writers elaborated the argument, and quoted authorities or used incidents to show tendency, precedent or motive, but Perdomo's note remains the clearest brief outline of the position.[9] The United States, he asserted, had always recognized the sovereignty of Santo Domingo. If this sovereign state increased its internal debt, there were legal means of deciding whether or not this violated the 1907 Convention, and the United States should have chosen these, not an assault upon the sovereignty of the weaker power. Domestic unrest did not give the United States any legal right whatever to interfere. Since no state of war existed between the countries, and there was nothing else to warrant such an armed aggression, the act was clearly contrary to the accepted principles of international law, and the aggrieved nation would vindivate its rights in due time.

There is no answer to this line of argument without denying the meaning it attaches to sovereignty. Senator Sumner had embarrassed the Grant administration by insisting that all sovereign states had equal rights, and that we could not excuse ourselves for threats against Haiti or Santo Domingo which we would not think of breathing against France because of her size. This matter of size and strength makes more difference in practice than it does in theory. Big states take an attitude toward little ones which would immediately provoke a fight between equals. In justifying themselves, the statesmen of these strong nations try to avoid the subject of sovereignty. Secretary Lansing's hasty telegram to Minister Russell, outlining Minister Perdomo's note and inquiring if he had been instructed by his Govern-

SETTING UP A MILITARY DICTATORSHIP 93

ment to write it, betrays a sudden fear lest the dispute had been successfully placed on the terrain of sovereignty, where all free nations are theoretically equal. Such was the case. When an official protest like this is lodged, it automatically goes to the world outside.

The strong nation in such a dispute appeals to precedent. Similar action has been taken before (citing cases), or a treaty has been grossly violated—the defendant goes into passages and precedents to prove that the terms used in the treaty have the meaning alleged. This part of Captain Knapp's proclamation of the Military Government was of course outlined in the State Department. Though carefully primed, he had himself just arrived, and was not personally familiar with the Dominican situation. His proclamation did not go into details about the alleged violations of the 1907 Convention. To do so would have been superfluous, as the intended readers in Santo Domingo already knew the American arguments, and rejected them. They were now assumed to be insincere as well as untenable, since the strong nation had refused to submit them to any disinterested third party. Since Captain Knapp's forces were already in possession, the excuses were a mere matter of form, and hardly filled the bill for the international lawyers.

Professor Philip Marshall Brown made some comments on the occupation[10] four months after it began which became the accepted statement of the American case outside the United States. The apology was quite brief, and some of the wording practically invited the sarcastic remarks with which Latin-America greeted it. Professor Brown admitted that the 1907 Convention had not "provided adequate safeguards for foreign creditors," and expressed the opinion that a "new treaty" would be "required." This would seem to admit that the "safeguards" the Americans were seeking by force were not actually covered by the existing treaty. The United States Government had based its insistent demands on the contrary assumption. If a "new treaty" was actually "required" in order to give us what we claimed, then obviously we were trying to get more than our existing treaty rights, and more, therefore, than any arbitrator on earth could have given us. Incidentally, this part of Professor Brown's analysis was correct, hard as it was on the explanations our State Department had been making. It was precisely Santo Domingo's refusal to sign a new and much stronger agreement which had led to our seizure of the country.

Professor Brown was not so clear in his identification of the "rebels" in the tilt between the President and his Congress in Santo Domingo. The Minister of War had "rebelled" against a President who had already violated the Constitution by an act of force. The Congress, which had proceeded to impeach President Jimenez in due constitutional fashion, would seem to have been the one party in the muddled situation which acted in an unquestionably legal way. Note that the fighting had been started by the President, who had attacked the capital, where the lawful Congress was impeaching him under the Constitution. We had not questioned the removal of President Morales a decade earlier, under similar circumstances. General Arias and his party, while perhaps "rebels," had tried to avoid a conflict. According to Professor Brown's version, the operations of "rebels" became "such a menace to American and foreign interests that the United States Marines were landed." By the "rebels," the Professor meant those sitting quietly in the fortress on the defensive, not the

SETTING UP A MILITARY DICTATORSHIP   95

makeshift army of an impeached President which precipitated the fighting.

These "rebels," we are told, continued to "fight on," attacking the United States Marine camp at "Monte Cristo" in June. Incidentally, there is no such place as "Monte Cristo" in Santo Domingo—the Professor must have had the French novel in mind. If it was "rebellion" for a group of native Dominicans to object to the landing of foreign troops at Monte Cristi, might we not apply the same term to the American defense of Washington against the British in 1814? What becomes of the glory of Joan of Arc, Kosciuszco and General Joffre? Anyhow, why "American and foreign interests"? What were the Americans but foreigners in Santo Domingo? Captain Knapp was logical. It is thinkable that such invasions are sometimes necessary, but what is the use of trying to make them "legal"?

The Professor's explanation of the "military law" instituted by the Americans in Santo Domingo was hardly comprehensible. It could not be martial law, as he admitted, for in American procedure, this applies "only in times of special emergency within the territorial jurisdiction of the United States." That the "military law" did "not apply to civilians" seemed to mean nothing at all in the face of the fact that it was freely applied to them. No Latin-American could see any sense in the proposition that a military government could be created without an "actual or implied state of war," based on the assumption that clashes and casualties do not constitute a "state of war" unless the strong power recognizes them as such.

Latin-America joyfully pulled this theoretical explanation of our conduct to pieces on the assumption that it was a defense. One is justified in wondering if it was really intended as such. Professor Brown held up the 1915 protectorate over Haiti as the "natural model to follow" in forcing our demands upon Santo Domingo. As far as Latin-America was concerned, this was equivalent to waving a red rag at a bull. A distinguished Cuban jurist[11] discussed the above explanation as a doctrine of the right of armed intervention to render diplomatic complaints effective, and pronounced it wholly untenable. It had been specifically repudiated by Spanish-American authorities such as Drago, by authorities and statesmen of the United States, by the Third Pan-American Conference at Rio Janeiro, and by the Second Hague Conference. In defense of the second part of this assertion, he quoted extensively from the addresses of Theodore Roosevelt and Elihu Root.

Especially did the Cuban jurist ridicule Professor Brown's declaration that there had been "no avowed hostile occupation," citing such cases as that of Captain Merckle, who committed suicide rather than stand trial on charges of systematic assassination. Why put in the word "avowed," thus seeming to make it a virtue not to face the unpleasant facts? This seventy-one page pamphlet, originally a speech before the Cuban International Law Society, is the kind of thing the world reads, and which cannot be entirely ignored. It was a real factor, among many, in bringing Santo Domingo's case to life after it had been buried by the distracting events of a war and a peace conference.

CHAPTER IX

THE REORGANIZATION OF SANTO DOMINGO, 1916-1922

"In Santo Domingo, the achievements of the military government have been highly creditable. . . . Critics who assume that the Dominican masses are opposed to American control are misinformed."—COLONEL G. C. THORPE, U. S. MARINE CORPS

. . . "A foreign military government conducted largely by officials who cannot speak the language of the people and who have no idea of their history or national psychology must necessarily be an unjust government."—SAMUEL GUY INMAN

. . . "The President of the United States, whoever he may be, disposes of the fortunes and shapes the destinies of the small countries bordering on the Caribbean Sea, according to his own and exclusive personal will; without a consistent and deliberate policy, without any knowledge or comprehension of the people of those countries, their problems, their needs, their woes, their aspirations; without any regard for international law; sometimes violating even the very elements of Christian civilization."—JACINTO LOPEZ

No careful observer can deny that the Military Government did some material good in Santo Domingo. So much propaganda was written about this, and so little that was not propaganda, that any sane estimate is very hard to make. Even the Dominican official publications were used by the Americans to sing their own praises. The only thing to do is to give a rough summary of the claims made by this official propaganda and offset it by indicating the side of the story which was carefully or ignorantly omitted.

According to the 1916 Receivership Report (p. 5), the assets in the sinking fund to cover the 1908 loan were $4,724,118.27. Besides the regular payments on that $20,000,000 loan, $360,000 a year of Dominican revenues had been going regularly to reduce the National City Bank loan of $1,500,000, which was within a year of final extinction at the time the Military Government was established. Due to the long deadlock, construction had been delayed, and a little over $3,000,000 in immediately available Dominican money had accumulated in the special public works fund. Besides this sum, the American occupation had held back most of the Dominican revenues for 1916. The Military Government thus had very important resources with which to make an initial showing.

The average expenditure by the Dominican Government for public works during the four years preceding 1916 was over twice the amount for that year, and far in excess of that for 1917. At first, that is to say, the Americans accumulated money by spending almost nothing on such needed improvements as roads. Prices had risen during 1915 and 1916, but they broke all records in 1917. Wartime inflation had quite as much to do with the vast increase in revenues as did the financial acumen of American military brains. The final payment on the National City Bank loan in 1917 freed Dominican finances from a very heavy load, leaving about a third of a million dollars available annually for other purposes. This would have taken place just the same—the intervention was not responsible for it.

A foreign military administration enjoys certain ad-

THE REORGANIZATION—1916-1922

vantages which the average civilian never thinks of, enabling it to make both a real and a fictitious showing. Suppose the British Navy were to take over the United States for a period, suppressing the whole mass of parliamentary salaries and the political "pork-barrel" which exists in all free countries. Besides doing this in Santo Domingo, the Americans supplied men drawing United States Navy pay for various high administrative positions. The country was policed in a similar way, avoiding most of a heavy bill for armed forces by transferring it to the unwitting American taxpayer. In the case of a big country, this fact could not be concealed. The British taxpayer would not and could not support a "benevolent" occupation of the United States.

Besides the outstanding public or bonded debt of a little over fifteen and a half millions of dollars at the end of 1916, there was a vague mass of claims, amounting to about the same figure if calculated at full face value. Much of this was inflated or spurious. Payments were suspended, and the whole was pared down by a commission to $4,292,343.52.[1] This was mainly expert civilian work, and the sum probably represented about the actual value of the claims. Santo Domingo thus owed some $20,000,000 above the amount in the sinking fund, but had over $3,000,000 in resources for public works besides various revenues withheld in 1916. At the 1915-1916 rate, which was increasing rapidly under wartime prices, the Receivership was building up a sinking fund of about $3,000,000 every five years. The scale-down of the floating indebtedness would necessarily have followed much the same course if the Dominican proposals had been accepted instead of imposing military rule, so the statistical summaries of the occupation's achievements at the time of the 1920 Presidential campaign were innocent or disingenuous to the extent of about $10,000,000 on this item alone.

Anyone who will take a little trouble to check through the Military Government's reports listed at the end of this chapter will see that very little had been done up to 1920 on public works. Lieutenant Commander Mayo, in charge of Finance and Commerce, listed a very imposing "Public works program."[2] adding up to $16,270,203.97. That almost none of this sum had been actually raised and spent early in 1920 is evident from the Navy Department's Memorandum dated August 5, 1921—over a year later.[3]

Even then, the sum claimed to have been applied to public works out of Dominican public funds was given in round numbers as "more than three and a half million dollars," which falls a good deal short of sixteen and a quarter millions. And the Military Government was in dire financial straits by that time. It was so flat broke, in fact, that it felt impelled to squirm out of an obligation of about a million dollars to the sugar planters, and began the year 1922 by issuing a certificate of indebtedness for $450,000.

According to pages 6-7 of the 1922 Receivership Report, the bonded debt of the Republic at the end of that year was as follows:

Outside Indebtedness,	1908 loan	....	$ 6,563,518.43
"	"	1918 "	$ 1,538,200.00
"	"	1922 "	$ 6,698,485.51

Total $14,800,203.94

The drop in the 1908 debt being arranged by a treaty and receivership antedating the Military Government, we can leave it out of our calculations. Over two and a half millions of dollars had been paid on the floating debt as fixed in the 1918 bond issue; but a new series of bonds for $6,700,000 had been issued in 1922. The old 1908 debt was not being reduced in 1916 at a rate of some $9,000,000 in five years. War prices and inflation played a certain role in the difference. A great deal of the expense of administration had also been removed by the suspension of free institutions.

It would not be possible accurately to calculate the cost of the adventure to the American taxpayer. We lost a cruiser, the *Memphis,* for which we had paid about $6,000,000. Consul C. B. Hosmer estimated the amount of American money spent in the Republic by the Forces of Occupation at "about $1,500,000 per annum."[4] If it was even two thirds of that, this item alone would have been $6,000,000 by the end of 1922. To these sums must be added such items as transportation, and the various stores and equipment sent from the United States to be used up in the enterprise.

The balance sheet is certain to remain largely a question of opinion. Even the material items cannot all be traced, and there are others in any social situation which evade all attempts to weigh them. There are some ways of organizing offices, including government bureaus, which are intrinsically better than others. Certainly the Americans introduced order and efficiency where inadequacy and even chaos had reigned. So it is with a system of military police. A disciplined force is a thousand times less dangerous than one which is little more than an armed mob. Coupled with regular and adequate pay, the discipline tends to make the trooper-policeman responsible, to place him above corruption and revolution. Add a road system so that the organized state can use this tool anywhere in its territories, and public order becomes possible. Highly disciplined police forces may become instruments of tyranny, but armed anarchy also has its drawbacks in this world of relative values.

Only one main highway had been completed in Santo Domingo when a provisional native government was set up in the fall of 1922. It ran from the capital about 180 miles northwest to Monte Cristi on the northern coast. There were other scraps of road, some bridges, improvements to trails, harbor works and public buildings as well. According to Minister Russell,[5] the Military Government completed 240 miles of first and second class road, and 155 of third class, the last generally meaning some work on existing trails. The total expense was $6,688,536. Of this, $3,770,000 was taken from current revenues and $2,917,918 borrowed.

This military occupation, which cost the American people a good many millions of dollars and Santo Domingo a considerable number of lives, upset the whole economic order of the latter country. Most of the high Naval and Marine officers had rather austere conceptions of their duty. They were not intentionally playing the game for private American business. As a general thing, the sugar planters were against the intervention and felt that it treated them badly. Foreign profits in such countries are likely to rest upon cheap land, cheap labor, high interest rates and a government which can be influenced. Contrary to a picture which used to be more or less current, interventions are usually brought about by bonded public debts, not purely private enterprises, or even concessions.

Swiftly running over the new measures adopted to raise money or simplify administration, we can see that the Military Government made endless trouble by being in too big a hurry. The old American-made tariff law of 1909 had enabled our Receivership to collect about ten dollars per capita annually in a country where most people barely found the necessities of life. Professor Fred R. Fairchild, of Yale University, reported to the Military Government in the winter of 1917-1918[6] that this system overtaxed necessities and generally tended to hamper economic development. The whole machinery of taxation was overhauled, including internal revenue.[7]

Internal revenue collections rose from $674,183.10 in the year the occupation began, to $1,697,163.23 in 1918, with only three months of the new law. During 1919, the first full year, the amount collected was $3,066,143.58, including $740,024.07 from the real property tax which went into effect July 1. One of the objects of this land tax was to force the registration of all titles, including share (*peso, comunero*) titles. The frank intention was to destroy collective holdings. An owner was practically obliged to improve his land in order to pay the tax. He usually wanted individual titles to a particular surface, rather than spend money in developing property which he shared with others. This measure was completed by a Land Registration Law of July 1, 1920,[8] the 146 articles of which looked forward to a uniform system of titles and the survey and division of all joint holdings. The main troubles with this land legislation were: First, it was impossible to collect or pay the heavy taxes, which were increased instead of lowered during the financial crisis beginning in 1920; second, such a general survey as division required would have taken many years and cost a vast sum,—in many cases more than the land was worth. Finally, the emphasis on clear, individual titles incidentally gave the sugar planters the opportunity they had sought for many years. The tax broke down almost entirely under its own weight, its yield dwindling to a very small sum by 1924—chiefly paid by the foreign sugar properties! In a word, it was a well-intentioned but thoroughly bungled mass of legislation.

When the sweeping tariff changes of 1919 were adopted, the Military Government was still dizzy with its own accomplishments and unaware that such inflation periods as had aided it have a way of coming to an end. The free list was very long. It included agricultural and industrial machinery and tools, means of transport and many kinds of building materials. Most coal and petroleum products were admitted free, gasoline paying a small tax of less than a cent a litre. This legislation was especially favorable to the big sugar concerns, which used much heavy machinery, as well as to American manufacturers, whose market was broadened.

Unfortunately, somebody has to pay revenues to maintain the government, even of a small country. Awaiting the sweeping reductions to take effect in 1920, importers cut down their orders late in 1919. Receipts were also abnormally low during that year because of a longshoremen's strike. Thus, much 1919 business was thrown over into 1920, enabling the Military Government to make a flattering but wholly misleading comparison of the two years. "Toward the end of the year" (1920), wrote the Customs Receiver,[9] "importers found themselves overstocked with millions of dollars worth of merchandise for which the peak of high prices had been paid, with a falling market as a barrier. During the year enormous quantities of textiles were imported, regardless of the limited demand and purchasing power of the country. . . . The natural result followed—paralysis of business."

"Food Control Order No. 10,"[10] issued by the Military Government in 1920, requisitioned about 8,000,000 pounds of sugar, to be held by the producers in their warehouses, at 17½ cents a pound. Orders 11 to 17 continued this arrangement for a year, while sugar prices were plunging to around 2 cents a pound. The loss was about a million dollars, finally paid by the sugar people under a threat to get it out of them by taxing their product. A tobacco purchase scheme of the Military Government was only a little less disastrous, but the burden fell upon the Dominican taxpayers in this case. For a Government to speculate in commodities like sugar and tobacco, at peak prices, would generally be considered a display of rather curious ideas of public finance. The *Gaceta Oficial* for June 29, 1921, two weeks after Rear-Admiral Robison had confidently announced the proposed American evacuation terms, printed Executive Order No. 641, setting aside $75,000 to clean up a school-desk tangle. These desks had been ordered at around $4 each under the Snowden-Mayo regime, and delivery accepted at $13.80 after a long delay. "At this rate," remarked the *Listin Diario* on July 1, "we will never pay off our debts."

Rear-Admiral Robison admitted in the *Listin Diario* for November 29, 1921, that the existing state of the finances made it "absolutely impossible to reduce or suspend the payment of the property tax," which the Dominicans had always gotten along without. M. Garcia Mella, a prominent attorney, stated in the same newspaper a month later that "the deficit of a million dollars which occurred during the past year was due to the mal-administration of the American Occupation." The issue of December 13 carried a cartoon entitled *Actualidad Dominicana*, showing a dismasted vessel marked "Treasury" drifting at the mercy of the waves, and poor *Concho Primo* (the Dominican) swimming among the sharks. Underneath, the wreck was attributed to the piloting of the Ship of State by "Marine Experts."

The Military Government got out of its immediate financial troubles in 1921-22 by loans, which the evacuation terms of course obligated Santo Domingo to assume. At the time of the final withdrawal in 1924, the land tax was already practically a dead letter. One of the first things Santo Domingo did on recovering her independence was to pass a series of taxes on "use, sale and consumption," which went a long way toward nullifying the terms of the 1919 tariff. These laws of 1925 can be most conveniently summarized later, in connection with their effects upon the sugar industry. What, then, was the net result of six years of full Marine occupation, down to the establishment of the Provisional Government in 1922? The one finished road represented a substantial beginning which has since assumed the proportions of a real system. Amateur financial policies by no means nullified all the good effects of orderly accounting in the Government bureaus. Financial difficulties toward the end hampered an excellent program of school reform, but did not entirely destroy it. The land title situation was improved, and may even be thoroughly reformed in the course of years. A very respectable, though quite general, geological survey was made. After all, the main trouble with the old Santo Domingo was chronic disorder. Inheritances from the incredibly bad Spanish colonial administration will inevitably hang on for a long time yet. Santo Domingo now has her first thoroughly disciplined police force, and a good beginning has been made toward a system of communications permitting the settlement of the interior and the maintenance of order everywhere. This road problem was exceptionally difficult, due to the mountainous nature of the country.

The main question is: Did these changes necessarily have to be accompanied by an unimaginative and sometimes brutal military occupation, and a vast growth of foreign property?

CHAPTER X

MILITARY JUSTICE FOR CIVILIANS

"True," quoted my Uncle Toby, "thou didst very right as a soldier, but certainly very wrong as a man."—LAURENCE STERNE

A SOLDIER is a man whose actions have been carefully mechanized. At bottom, he may be as human as any other person, but part of his humanity is suspended. Shooting to kill is often deemed essential to his authority and safety. It is not murder, for it is not against the law, established by his superiors. Military rule cannot bear criticism. A rigid censorship was declared with the occupation of Santo Domingo in 1916, and elaborated from time to time by orders and decrees. The provost courts were "composed of one or more American officers and were originally established to take cognisance of 'offenses against the military government,' but this phrase was stretched to cover almost anything."[1]

Colonel Thorpe stated in 1920 that 116 "distinct fights or skirmishes" between Marines and Dominicans had taken place, resulting in 55 American casualties and "many times our aggregate" on the other side. Armed opposition is the first and most obvious class of "offenses." There were at least three other types over which the American military courts kept rigid jurisdiction: The carrying or ownership of arms or explosives without a permit; the sale of alcoholic drink to Marines;

and the making of any remark, verbally or in print, regarded by the Military Government as uncomplimentary to itself—sufficiently so that it "tended" to incite to "unrest, disorder and revolt." This "tendency" being purely a matter for the military court to decide, it did not need to be very strong.

As a rule, a case involving arms was simple enough. Either the accused had them, without a permit, or he did not. A sale of liquor was often more complicated. Marines would send civilians after the forbidden beverages, and it was often a question whether the merchant had any way of knowing the destination. When Americans demanded liquor with arms in their hands, the proprietor was sometimes the only Dominican witness. If he refused, he could be charged with trying to *sell* liquor; or, if his place were out of the crowded ways, much worse might happen to him immediately. For example, one Luis Bautista, of Guayabo Dulce, had his store burned down by Marines on the evening of December 26, 1920, because an employee had refused to sell them liquor. Shots were fired to prevent anyone from putting out the blaze. Several other stores and houses were then burned for the same reason. Some Marines got prison sentences for this crime. Bautista himself, besides losing $7,000 by the fire, was fined $3,000 (later reduced to $500) and spent eleven months in prison—on the testimony of this group of soldiers![2]

Before taking up the cases of *sedition*(!) which were the most interesting, one disagreeable comment is necessary on Colonel Thorpe's assertion that no native had paid the price of capital punishment. A number of Dominicans—we may be certain that nobody knows exactly how many—were put to death offhand by the Marines, and some were tortured, without ever having had their day in court at all. The assassinations by Captain Merckle were repudiated by his superiors, and he committed suicide while awaiting trial. Repudiation of the few which were found out does not, unfortunately, bring the dead back to life, or restore the silhouettes of burned villages against the sky. A number of Merckle's atrocities were described by eye-witnesses before the Senate Committee.[3]

Dr. Coradin, of Hato Mayor, testified that he had seen two men killed offhand. One of them, a man eighty years old, had first been dragged at the tail of a horse. The other "appeared to have made some remarks that offended Captain Merckle," whereupon the officer "took him to a corner of the house, drew his revolver, and shot him in the left ear." These are only samples of the cases recited. Emilio Saurez, drafted as a guide in April, 1918, described such tortures as cutting off ears, burning a wounded leg, and putting acid fruit juice in slashes made in a man's chest.

All resistance was "banditry" to the Marines, even when it was organized, using flags and uniforms. The Vicentico case was a famous one of an actual bandit and murderer who was enticed by false promises of a police job to come over to the Marine side of the argument. He was then put in irons, and later shot by a Marine officer, ostensibly for "trying to escape." Perhaps he deserved the treachery and assassination which he himself had practiced, but that was, after all, not exactly what we sent our civilizing mission to Santo Domingo for.

There were many cases of the prosecution of journalists, public speakers and well-known writers. The suppression of newspapers occurred almost innumerable times, from 1916 to 1922. One article was censored for mentioning the name of Emmanuel Kant, because he was a German! An official address of the Chief Justice of Santo Domingo was blue-penciled. A provost court sentenced a man for five years at hard labor—later committed to banishment—because he had circulated a book by the speaker of the Porto Rican House of Delegates. A Spanish priest spent five months in an infamous calaboose in Samana because he had mentioned the efficiency of the German army, in a table conversation, long before the United States had entered the war.[4]

We can probably get a better idea of the workings of the military courts and the military mind by dealing with one case in some detail than by merely listing a number. Fabio Fiallo's is a particularly good example. This poet and man of state, known for his writings wherever Spanish is read, kindly lent the writer a complete typewritten transcript of his trial, made by the American Military Court itself and furnished to the accused on his demand.

Edith Cavell, condemned to death by a German military court, was undoubtedly "guilty," and subject to the penalty imposed. Mata Hari, the lovely Javanese dancer who was put to death by the French, was also guilty, according to military law. Yet the French case was hardly noticed, and the Germans were reviled from one end of the world to the other. The difference was mainly one of imagination and tact, guilt or innocence under military law having practically nothing to do with it. The Fabio Fiallo affair was America's Cavell case. To most Americans, the "poet patriot" was a passing headliner in the press, but his trial in 1920 made the *"Yankees"* about as loathsome as possible to the Latin peoples of the two hemispheres. In fact, relatively little fuss was made over the Cavell case in Latin countries, and a great deal over Fabio Fiallo. The woman was clearly guilty of a major military offense, committed in the interest of a great power, in wartime. At least it took courage and conviction to execute her. The poet had committed a journalistic indiscretion, in peacetime, in the interest of a weak nation occupied by foreign soldiery. Better known as poet and scholar, Fabio Fiallo had also found time to taste public life, having been both a Minister of State and a provincial governor. He is one of those occasional men so handsome that it is a genuine handicap to them. One look at his picture in stripes, which was circulated all over Latin America and Europe, did more to convey what the Dominicans wanted thought about the American Military Government than a million chosen words could do or undo. This was not the intention of the officers of the military court. Justice to them was stern; they were sentimental about the metal balances in her right hand.

Manuel Flores Cabrera owned a daily newspaper in Santo Domingo City called *Las Noticias*. He was glad to have noted literary and public men like Fabio Fiallo, Americo Lugo, and Enrique Henriquez write articles for his paper, which they did free as a medium for their views. Fabio Fiallo was called *Director-Redactor*, a kind of literary chairman common in Spanish countries. He was in no way responsible for the work of the others, entitled to reject it, or even obligated to read it.

During the summer of 1920, some leading Dominicans conceived the idea of a "Patriotic Week," in which particular efforts should be made to call the attention of the outside world to the country's grievances. Fabio Fiallo was one of a few public men in a country of revolutions, where "generals" were about as thick as "colonels" in the United States, who had never sought any military title or taken part in a revolt. "We had no purpose whatever," he stated at his trial, "to stir the people to revolt, which would have been nothing short of criminal, in view of their defenseless condition." What they did hope to do was to draw the attention of Latin America to Santo Domingo's plight. They succeeded much better than they had intended!

Lugo wrote an article entitled "La Semana Patriotica" ("Patriotic Week") which appeared July 6, charging the United States of North America with the demolition of Dominican institutions and liberty. A week later, Fabio Fiallo wrote a strong appeal to his countrymen to drop their troubles with each other. His language concerning the one type of Dominican he did not want for a friend was rather flamboyantly Spanish. This undesirable citizen, as the *Director-Redactor* saw the matter, was the catspaw of the foreign invader—prosperous in his new connection and sneering in his attitude toward the cruder days of independence. The poet used such expressions as "martyrdom of the fatherland," "chains," "outrages," and "this cruel civilization which came to us through the back door with fixed bayonets in a dark night of deceit, surprise and cowardice. . . ."

If a Belgian had written such a squib during the German occupation, he might very well have been shot, instead of threatened with that penalty. Latin America took the public threat as an announcement of intention. That the poet was not actually put to death was generally attributed to the storm of resolutions, protests and petitions showered upon President Wilson.

Fabio Fiallo was charged with two violations of Executive Order No. 385, signed January 15, 1920, and published in the *Gaceta Oficial* six days later. This order had ostensibly abolished the press censorship, but had vaguely prohibited the setting forth of doctrines "tending" to incite the masses to "unrest, disorder and revolt," or to show "the present condition of Santo Domingo in a way manifestly unjust or false, and which might provoke disorder among the masses." Since a foreign military court was to be the sole judge of the tendency to provoke revolt—which did not have to be a probability—the order was all-comprehensive in case of need. Even "scorn, obloquy and ridicule" were not forgotten, though always associated with a "tendency" to "create disorder or revolt." The queerest thing about all this language and its interpretation was a sentence in the Executive Order stating quite clearly and grammatically: "The rights of assembly and free speech shall not be interfered with except as necessary to preserve order."

From the civilian point of view, this trial was a farce. The poet's well-known and publicly expressed views against armed resistance were objected to as evidence by the Second-Lieutenant who acted as Judge Advocate, and ruled out by the court. No evidence concerning the "tendency" to provoke unrest was admitted. This was held to be a question for the court to decide. There was absolutely nothing that the defendant could do, once he had admitted authorship of one article and identified himself as the *"Director-Redactor"* referred to. The word "Redactor" was found in Webster's Dictionary, and its English definition coupled to that of the English word "Director" to get the meaning of the hyphenated expression! What the title meant in practice, in a Spanish country, was held by the Court to be immaterial. Under Dominican law, a man cannot be tried for a collection of offenses at once, but only for the most serious. Neither can an alleged accomplice be tried, under most Latin codes, until his principal has been convicted. The Judge Advocate retorted when these points were raised that the special military tribunal was not bound by the Dominican penal code of laws, Anglo-Saxon civil law, or even by Naval laws, by which it was merely "guided."

Lieutenant-Commander Mayo, the propagandist who got the Military Government into the produce markets to the tune of a couple of millions, was called in to read columns of figures as "proof" that the articles were "manifestly unjust and false." The Second-Lieutenant who served as Judge Advocate or prosecutor quoted the printed wisdom of Colonel Constantine M. Perkins on military law to the President of the court—Colonel Constantine M. Perkins! Colonel Perkins believed that such "courts" were merely "advisory committees" to assist the commander in rooting out the facts, and "likewise soothe his conscience as to the punishment inflicted." Colonel Thorpe tried to make the Clark University Conference believe, in 1920, that this was like an American court at home. Perhaps he meant a police court, or a traffic court.

There is one nice Latin distinction which the defense kept insisting upon, and which was entirely wasted upon the prosecution and the court. "Obedience" and "loyalty" to an authority are not the same thing. It is clear to a Latin mind that a man can be loyal only to what he believes in. A government—even a military one, founded on force alone—can exact a certain outward obedience, but it cannot make people love it. The more the American Military Government of Santo Domingo tried with soldiers, words and columns of figures to make Dominicans regard it with a tearful gratitude to match its sense of its own benevolence, the more anxious they became to get rid of it. Latin America did not feel that even disobedience had been proved against Fabio Fiallo. His three-year sentence (later shortened to one) and heavy fine were seized upon as an act of tyrannical spitework, meted out by a gang of Cossacks because they could not break his will.

Fabio Fiallo's guilt or innocence are of no more consequence than Edith Cavell's. His tormentors merely threatened the extreme penalty that hers had the courage to carry out, gave him a mock trial which only served to convince neutral opinion that the man ought to have a medal, and shut him up in an old Spanish prison, pictures of which were scattered over the world. One Spanish magazine displayed a half-tone of New York harbor, with the Statue of Liberty looking down upon it at the top of the page. Fabio Fiallo, the "poet patriot," was shown in stripes at the right, and on the left was a picture of the peasant Cayo Bayez, whose bared breast showed the scars left by hot bayonets. The text which filled up the odd spaces on this page did not leave much to the imagination.

Max Henriquez y Ureña went to Europe, where he spoke, to crowded halls, of American brutality. Fabio's book of verses *Canciones de la Tarde*, which had just appeared, had an enormous sale. *Le Journal*, of Paris, compared him with Tagore, and the *Revue Diplomatique* mentioned him as one of the great literary men of the Spanish language. *La Prensa*, of Havana, carried a typical Latin-American article August 4, 1920, bitterly railing at a country which could boast of putting down Hohenzollern tyranny and at the same time invade the West Indies as "civilizing conquerors," clapping poets into jail.

A presidential campaign was on in the United States.

Fabio Fiallo was released. The Military Government had not learned anything. It had justified the conviction in the *Listin Diario* of Santo Domingo, August 24, by affirming that "the officer who establishes martial law is at once supreme legislator, supreme judge and supreme executive." Somewhat bewildered by their misadventure with Fabio Fiallo, these supreme legislators passed stiffer laws: Executive Order No. 572, on *sedition,* and No. 573, on *slander.*[5] They did little but split the old Executive Order No. 385 into two parts, stop a few loopholes and provide heavy penalties, including both fines and imprisonment. These orders were quite unworkable, and were both repealed a month later.

Some suppressions and prosecutions of newspapers took place as late as 1922, but there was little heart in them after Fabio Fiallo's release. Negotiations for withdrawal went on from December, 1920, until July, 1921, and were resumed after the Senate investigation at the end of the year. In October, the *Listin Diario* published depositions describing alleged outrages committed by one Captain Bockalaw in the outlying province of Espaillat—similar to those of Captain Merckle three years earlier. At the end of October, a detachment of Marines collected and marched out all the male members of the commune of Los Llanos. These things were publicly denounced by Fabio Fiallo as "acts of blood and brutality." The Los Llanos affair, defended by Rear-Admiral Robison as necessary, was naturally compared by the Dominicans with German and Turkish concentrations of civilians during the war.

Banditry was exceptionally bad in 1921, in spite of the expensive constabulary. Ramon Reyes was kidnapped from the Las Pajas sugar plantation, August 27. Thomas J. Steel, manager of the Angelina property, was taken from his house September 28, and held for $5,000 ransom.

The Military Government's land legislation had been used with great energy by some of the sugar concerns to get legal title to huge tracts of land. Central Romana, for example, now owned the sites of some Dominican villages. Emilio A. Morel, of the town of La Romana, protested publicly to the Attorney General on August 8 that the sugar company had given evacuation notice to the populations of Caimoni and Higueral. The two places were to be destroyed. A letter dated four days later appeared, like the first, in the *Listin Diario*. The heading used was: "The Crime is Consummated." Both villages had been burned, and a hundred and fifty families were out under the sky. Morel remarked that William Bass, an American sugar man of Macoris, had been prosecuted and imprisoned for a similar offense under a Dominican Government years before.

A military occupation has to adopt standards of conduct and legal procedure which would be atrocious on the part of a civil government. The civil population concerned is often perfectly honest in failing to see the distinction. Even if there had been no such episodes as torturings with firebrands or the promiscuous "bumping off" (Marine jargon for killing) of people without trial in out of the way places, the charge of Cossack methods would have been inevitable. The only sure way to escape this kind of unsavory publicity is to avoid military occupations.

CHAPTER XI

GETTING RID OF THE MARINES

Si Inquieren por nosostros:—Son felices?—Decidles
Los vimos en cadenas vencidos a traición . . .
Mustias están sus frentes, sus brazos abatidos,
Y en sus pechos no caben más odio y más dolor.
FABIO FIALLO

"I know it to be a fact that nine-tenths of the Dominicans are in favor of the military occupation. There are professional politicians who would like to see us recalled home because they want to get their hands in the Public Treasury. But they are going to be disappointed."—REAR-ADMIRAL SNOWDEN

REAR-ADMIRAL SNOWDEN'S statement, as quoted by Sarah MacDougall in the *New York Times*, October 10, 1920, was reprinted in the *Listin Diario* of Santo Domingo on December 15. Its truth was challenged. The paper expressed a disbelief that even *one percent* of the natives favored a continuation of the regime. In order to forestall the charge that it was the poor who favored Marine rule, the *Listin Diario* offered to pay the expenses of any such people who wished to appear in the capital before the American Senatorial Commission. This had no effect on the monotonous uniformity of the attitude expressed. Judge Schoenrich could well say that there was hardly a Dominican but was glad to see the Marines go.

Even the American Customs Receivership, which was almost purely technical and had done its work with great competency, especially during the two periods before 1913 and after 1920 when it was under Mr. Pulliam's direction, got on Santo Domingo's nerves. After all, it was *Yanqui*. In 1921, Fabio Fiallo clouded its origins by dumping into the daily press a series of quotations from official documents concerning the expenses of Velasquez and Dr. Hollander back in 1906-08.[1] It was Velasquez that Fabio was trying to get at. In resurrecting the old question of Hollander's huge fee (accepted from Santo Domingo after the State Department had already paid him once) and the curious method of collecting it, the obvious intention was to make Velasquez responsible, if not to hint that he had shared the money. The writer interviewed many public men in Santo Domingo in 1926, among whom the attitude toward the Receivership seemed pretty uniform. As one put it, the institution might have done good in the past; Mr. Pulliam was a nice fellow, who deserved to be happy in the Philippines, where it was to be hoped he would soon return!

Francisco J. Peynado, Ex-Minister to Washington and Minister of Finance in 1916, bore the brunt of the negotiations for American evacuation. Testifying before the Senate Commission December 10, 1921,[2] he expressed the opinion that the thing for the United States to do was "to give us our independence with the security of your friendship." He said frankly that he believed his own Government had acted legally in 1916, the Americans arbitrarily and illegally. Foreign property had not been menaced by the revolutions, and foreign lives were far safer in Santo Domingo than in New York. Dr. Peynado could recall only one case of an American losing his life. This had occurred in 1885, purely by accident, and an indemnity of $33,000 had been exacted.

The thirty-page Peynado memorandum[3] was sent to the Commission under date of January 4, 1922, and published at the same time. It began by presenting the case against the Military Government, and explaining why the American 1920-21 move toward evacuation had been rejected.[4] The Dominicans had been faced in 1921 with terms similar to those of Minister Russell's famous Note No. 14, presented in November, 1915. They had struck at the first, fourth and fifth of the five general items. The other two merely validated a $2,500,000 loan and brought payments on it under the supervision of the General Receiver of Customs.

Article I of the American proposal of 1921 called for a ratification of *all* the acts of the Military Government. This went through in the agreement finally adopted in 1922, with the exception of a few "face-savers"—unimportant items which the Americans could afford to concede. Article IV called for an extension of the Customs Receiver's functions to internal revenues. This the Dominicans rejected and the Americans had to concede the point. The final proposition, also killed by Dominican opposition, was the old one of 1915 for an American officered constabulary, paid and invested with "proper and adequate authority" by Santo Domingo.

The Military Governor had made a very bad break in July, 1921, practically threatening that his Government would do nothing more until the Dominicans came to the terms laid down. After the Senate Investigation at the end of the year, there were two sets of terms, one American and one Dominican. Peynado thought that the Americans should do something about the economic crisis, for which he blamed the Military Government; thus handing the country back to its owners with its finances in tolerable working order. The items he particularly insisted upon were: the correction of the unworkable features of the 1919 tariff, and the extension to Santo Domingo of the tariff preferences given Cuba.

Under the 1919 tariff, the customs receipts for 1921 fell lower than at any time since the early days of the Receivership. Peynado charged that the measure neither produced adequate revenues nor fostered the development of national industries. Of two hundred and forty-five articles put on the free list and seven hundred more paying low duties, nearly all favored American products. Not only was there no genuine reciprocity, but Santo Domingo was prevented by the Convention of 1907 from making reciprocal tariff agreements with other countries. Dominican industries such as leather, tobacco, coffee and cocoa found their protection reduced or abolished. The only agricultural product favored by the American-made tariff of 1919 was sugar—a foreign-owned industry. It was further aided by the abolition of duties on such machinery as was not required by other agricultural enterprises. The only reduction on sugar duties was on the grades imported by the richer people—largely foreigners—from the United States. The abolition of duty on coffee had brought the Brazilian product into the Dominican market.

In 1919, under the old tariff, only $349,677 worth of shoes had been imported. During 1920, these imports jumped to $1,555,801, of which 98 percent came from the United States, Porto Rico and the Virgin Islands. A promising industry in Santo Domingo was ruined. The removal of the duty on machinery did little to help the small scale shoemaker, faced with a reduction of 40 to 60 percent in the tariff on shoes.

In attacking Rear-Admiral Robison's explanation of the financial troubles,[5] Peynado correctly calculated the sugar requisition as a valid and loyal obligation, though it was later repudiated by the Military Government. Including this, the actual deficit for 1921 was over $2,000,000. The original public works reserve fund of $3,000,000 had been entirely dissipated, without the completion of a single main road (up to May, 1922). Nor does Peynado forget that the invaders had not been obliged to pay an army, representatives or senators. Robison had claimed that the Military Government's anticipated loan of $10,000,000 had been frustrated by the "disapproval and protests" of the Dominican people, leaving a vast lot of beginnings hanging in the air at the end of 1920. Forgetting all about the world-wide financial crisis, particularly bad in Santo Domingo, the Rear-Admiral blamed the political agitation of 1921 for the dizzy fall in the yield of the land tax. Peynado's general retort was to the effect that it was the Military Government's own lack of foresight which had gotten it into financial straits and that the ruinous terms of a loan contracted at the worst possible time fell upon the Dominicans, not the Americans.

The actual history of the land tax shows that it worked only during the inflation period. It yielded $1,011,002.09 in 1920, dropping to $532,295.28 in 1921, and less than $350,000 in 1924 and 1925, even including a new school tax on land begun in 1922. Official figures for 1924, furnished the writer by the Department of Commerce and Finance, show that the sugar estates paid 56 percent of it. They claimed they paid 95 percent.

"The Memorandum of the Agreement of Evacuation," dated June 30, 1922,[6] was negotiated at Washington by Dr. Peynado, Frederico Velasquez (for the *Progresista* party), General Horatio Vasquez (for the *Nacional* party), and Elias Brache (for the *Liberal* party). Peynado was the only one of the informal commission who spoke English. It was charged in Santo Domingo that Peynado let the State Department dictate the terms, the other members being mere figureheads. He did not get either his Cuban rates or any modification of the 1919 tariff law.

These four negotiators and Archbishop Nouel (who was added by unanimous agreement) chose a Provisional President and Cabinet. As soon as this Provisional Government was inaugurated in the fall of 1922, the Marines were concentrated at a few places. With American "advisors," the new hand-picked group of Dominicans proceeded to arrange the "necessary amendments" to the constitution and laws—as meticulously specified in the memorandum already prepared at Washington. Sumner Welles, former Chief of the Latin-American Division of the Department of State, was sent down as a special American Commissioner.

Juan Bautista Vicini Burgos took a curious oath of office as Provisional President.[7] He announced the names of a Cabinet and declared all the standing American Executive Orders and Resolutions, Administrative Regulations and Contracts in force until legislative bodies could be provided.

Both customs and internal revenue receipts rose enormously during 1923, and again in 1924. It is not recorded that the Provisional Government followed the Mayo precedent by crediting its own astuteness with the increase.[8] Expenses also mounted, as people on the

GETTING RID OF THE MARINES

American Navy payroll were replaced by Dominicans. A congress was elected in the fall of 1923.

General Horatio Vasquez won the Presidency in the spring election of 1924, by a coalition of his *Nacionalistas* with the *Progresista* party of Frederico Velasquez. A Constituent Assembly adopted a new Constitution in harmony with the hundreds of Military Government orders, regulations and contracts, and the specifications of the Washington agreement of 1922. The new instrument was signed and proclaimed June 13, 1924.[9] It reestablished the Vice-Presidency (which had been abolished in 1908), thus taking care of Velasquez in the coalition. He was named for the office. The last Marines left within two months of the Velasquez inauguration on July 12. Before the end of the year, all the ratifications of the 1922 Evacuation Agreement had taken place. Santo Domingo was again as nearly independent as in 1916.

There are several curious provisions in this 1924 constitution, including the prohibition of capital punishment, export taxes and the issue of paper money. The standard currency is the American dollar. No foreigner can belong to the constabulary—this finally putting to sleep one of the persistent American proposals. Peaceful succession to the presidency is elaborately provided for. The armed forces can never have any deliberative functions, but must obey the Government at all times.

One of the first moves of the new Government was a surprise and a disappointment to the former tutors. During 1924, the Customs Receiver and the American Commissioner had worked out a scheme for a new $25,-000,000 loan. This was intended to refund all outstanding obligations and furnish some $10,000,000 for public works.[10] The loan was finally rejected on the ground that it would extend the Receivership for some years.

The refusal of the loan practically nullified a new customs convention signed at Washington, December 27, 1924. According to this arrangement, Santo Domingo was to pay on her bonded debt only 10 percent of the customs receipts in excess of $4,000,000 instead of *half* the surplus above $3,000,000 as provided in the 1907 Convention. Three millions was too small a basis with the greatly diminished purchasing power of gold in 1924; and as a result the debt was being paid off too rapidly, leaving insufficient revenue to run the government. Besides increasing the face of the Dominican debt, it was proposed to reduce the rate of payment. This would naturally add years to the life of the American Customs Receivership. The Dominicans refused, preferring to be poor for a time and get out of debt.[11] Up to 1926 at least, the Receiver continued to collect and pay according to the 1907 schedule.

At the end of 1925, the net outstanding indebtedness of Santo Domingo, deducting sinking fund assets from bonds due, was $11,174,545.42. The 1918 loan was paid off during that year.[12] At the rate of payment from 1924 to 1926, the whole debt could be extinguished before 1935. As far as we can see, this would mean the premature end of the Receivership. That is the way the Dominicans rather light-heartedly view the matter.

Santo Domingo's American tutors got even a ruder jar than the rejection of the $25,000,000 loan in a series of tax laws passed during 1925.[13] These are ostensibly internal revenue acts. In practice, they are vast modifications of the tariff of 1919. Law 190 itself, passed in May, 1925, taxed the sale and use of a comparatively short list of goods, and was important only because of the precedent established. Since Dominican produce was formally exempted, the act was merely a tariff in disguise.

What the Americans who cry out against "Law 190" really mean is Law No. 278 signed by President Vasquez November 24, 1925. Its single article declared No. 190 amended by extending the tax to cover "articles, effects and merchandise which may be introduced into the country after the promulgation of this Law, and which shall de declared for *use, sale* or *consumption* [italics mine] in accordance with the following rates: . . ." The heading of the list of 202 items, some of them covering whole classes of goods, is: "Sales, Use and Consumption Tax."

While the list is quite too long to reproduce here, it may be remarked that the tax falls upon the very goods favored by the Military Government in its 1919 tariff. That law itself was put beyond amendment during the lifetime of the loans by the terms of the evacuation agreement. Among the things now heavily taxed are many characteristic imports of the sugar concerns, and manufactures coming especially from the United States. We may mention gasoline, automotive equipment, shoes, refined sugar, cottonseed oil, rubber tires, cement, lubricants, iron and steel for construction, railway material, lumber, cotton goods and a great many kinds of machinery. A comparison of the list with that of America's exports to Santo Domingo[14] will give an idea of how thoroughly Law No. 278 serves the purpose of a protective tariff against goods from the United States.

It is even more important as a producer of revenue, but the revenue comes largely from resident foreigners.[15] The Dominican Government had tested the attitude at Washington with a pretty clear, though not at all open or defiant, violation of the evacuation terms, and nothing had happened.

CHAPTER XII

SUGAR—A CASE OF INDUSTRIAL FEUDALISM

In Cuba it is difficult to find lands at any price, while in Santo Domingo the richest portion of the country has not been touched, and lies ready and willing for the hand of the farmer or the dollar of the capitalist to make it produce for the benefit of mankind and especially the Dominicans.—*Libro Azul* ("Bluebook") *of 1920*

ECONOMIC penetration by outsiders went on in Santo Domingo on a small scale before the introduction of steam sugar mills following 1870; but the foreign business of today has grown up mainly around this one industry. None of the great banks now operating in the country appeared there until after the sugar business was fairly mature. The case is the same with development of import trade, which was insignificant up to the period under discussion.

Although the earlier ventures were begun by individuals, this stage has been outgrown during the past twenty years. The cane sugar business, though it takes its own raw material from agriculture, is a typical heavy machine industry. Under present-day conditions, economy of production calls for a million-dollar mill, and the mill itself represents only a fraction of the total capital required. The plant is useful only a few miles from enough cane to keep it grinding during a season of four to six months. To clear land and bring cane to maturity on a big tract adds enormously to the initial capital investment before there are any returns. Widely fluctuating prices for the finished product add hazard to what would be a good deal of a gamble in any case.

During the period of years before actual production begins, the costs may pile up in a quite unpredictable way. For example, the Barahona enterprise, launched in 1916, was first hit by the wartime rise in machinery prices and labor. This plantation is irrigated. Salt seepage developed soon after the water was turned on, requiring an expensive drainage system and spoiling some of the fields, at least for a period of years. Maintenance is particularly costly, heavy machinery being used so far from its place of manufacture that elaborate repair facilities have to be available on the ground. Finally, a big plantation requires an extensive railway system. This problem may be a really maddening one if the land lies badly and the hauls are fairly long.

Cane sugar early became strictly a rich man's game. From this stage it passed into one of vast corporations, few men caring to tackle it alone, no matter what their wealth. The Cuban Dominican Sugar Company will serve to illustrate the structure of such concerns, which interlock in a way suggesting nothing else so much as a feudal system.

Down to 1924, when it was dissolved, the West India Sugar Finance Corporation was listed in the literature of the Bureau of Foreign and Domestic Commerce as the New York purchasing agent for a number of concerns in Santo Domingo. After 1924, the Cuban Dominican Sugar Company replaced the older corporation in such lists and was presently named as the purchasing agent for two additional mills. If we turn to *Moody's Industrials*[1] we discover that some of the properties were incorporated separately, and that the Department of

Commerce literature had not told us much about the real ownership. The American Government gets its information from consular personnel and Trade Commissioners, who often have no way of knowing any more than they report. *Moody's Industrials,* if the issues for several years are consulted, shows one Thomas A. Howell to have been prominent in both of the above corporations, figuring as President, Vice-President, Director, and President of the Board.

Looking back through various issues of the *New York Directory of Directors,* we find Mr. Howell in a number of corporations: a member of the firm of B. H. Howell, Son & Company, a Director of the Second National Bank of the City of New York, Trustee of another bank, and Director in a string of sugar concerns, including the Cuban American, and Barahona.

Associated with Mr. Howell, as directors of the same corporations, we find many other people. Among the recurring names is that of Mr. J. H. Post, member of the Howell firm, Director of the National City Bank, sometime President and Director of the National Sugar Refining Company, Director of the West India Sugar Finance Corporation, and so on, at great length.

The Cuban Dominican Sugar Company has often been mentioned as a "National City concern." This does not mean that the National City Bank owns it, or that identically the same people own both. Of the fifteen Directors of the Cuban Dominican mentioned in *Moody's Industrials* for 1926, only three names appear in the National City Bank list given in the *Directory of Directors.* Of the remaining twelve, some are Directors in other banks, including the Guaranty Trust, National Park, U. S. Trust and Chemical National; but the National City is the only case of more than one.

This feudal empire of sugar has highly intricate ramifications, not all of which can be calculated. The fifteen Cuban Dominican Directors often come together in other sugar companies, including mills, refineries and manufactories of machinery. Another common link is steamship companies. Sometimes a man will have only the one sugar connection, being in a different kind of business with other persons already directors or former directors. This is not the only overlapping—that of stockholders is almost impossible to trace.

Banks do not usually play the role in economic penetration which the popular imagination often attributes to them. An investment bank makes money for its stockholders by selling the use of capital at the highest possible interest and dividend rates consistent with safety. For example, a man named Hatton had the idea of starting an irrigated sugar plantation in Barahona. He and his brother had inherited the San Isidro estate, over-expanded it, bought too much machinery, and lost the property. It went to the Bartram Brothers, butter dealers of New York, who had been drawn into tropical transport, mill supplies, etc. . . . They added the Consuelo estate, which the Bass family had likewise over-developed. Hatton had some money left. Preliminary surveys and investigations had to be made at Barahona in order to convince big sugar people that the project was an engineering possibility. It was also necessary to get some kind of an option on the land. The Barahona Company was organized with a New York charter in 1916. Among the people involved was H. J. Pulliam. He was Secretary, Treasurer, and a Director of the Kelly firm which owned the Ansonia plantation at Azua, also an irrigated property, and not far from Barahona. Pulliam was in the West India Finance Corporation, and

SUGAR—INDUSTRIAL FEUDALISM

also a beet sugar concern, the Western Sugar and Land Company. He was on directorates with various members of the Board of the later Cuban Dominican.

The Barahona Company ran into unexpected expenses and required more money before it arrived at full production. By 1920, the International Banking Corporation, a National City concern in the strict sense, had been in Santo Domingo three years, and was a natural source of some of the needed funds. In that year, the Cuban Dominican Sugar Development Syndicate was organized, at the height of the sugar boom, to take over some going concerns and also to furnish capital to several needy ones, including Barahona. The oldest of these interlocking firms was the West India Sugar Finance Corporation. It had existed as a Connecticut corporation before the World War, to finance growing crops. Recall that its membership was pretty much everybody in sugar. It took mortgages, liens, etc., on properties to protect its investments, and sometimes took over the management, but was not designed as a permanent owner of plantations.

In 1920, the Finance Corporation had two Cuban properties (Santa Ana and Haitillo) on its hands. The Barahona project needed a lot of money for completion. Bartram Brothers wanted to sell their two paying estates, San Isidro and Consuelo. The Cuban Dominican Sugar Development Syndicate was organized to finance the whole. Barahona was already incorporated in New York, but the mill now became a separate Dominican corporation. This was due to American taxes and also to some Dominican laws. One corporation was set up for the two Cuban properties and the Bartram estates were incorporated in Santo Domingo as the Compañia Azucarera Dominicana. Note that not a single *mill* was put under American laws *and taxes*, but that *Dominican* land was held by the same people under a New York charter.

Sugar took its dizzy drop from over twenty cents a pound to less than a tenth of that figure soon after the above financial operation. Lieutenant-Commander Mayo's requisition held millions of pounds out of the market during the debacle,—after which he forced the mill people to take the loss. In the spring of 1921, the American duty was raised from 1.256 cents to 2 cents a pound, and the next fall to 2.206 cents. This last figure was about five-sevenths of the average price in Santo Domingo during 1921. Very likely the world's sugar could be produced at around 3½ cents a pound outside the American tariff, under the general price level of 1921, but the readjustment was too sudden. The cost and capitalization of mills, land prices and rents, contracts for cane, etc., were mainly based on at least twice as much. Land can be used to grow ten cent sugar which could never be made to pay costs at 3 or 4 cents. A high price is like a tariff in that it brings unsuitable land under cultivation, leads to over-capitalization, and so on.

Both the 1924 and the 1926 "refinancing" operations of the Cuban-Dominican group represent hard times as well as extension. Instead of low prices cutting production in the cane sugar business, they often do just the opposite. The main apparent reason why sugar refuses to follow any moderately simple "economic laws" is the combination of a tremendous initial investment with a long wait (during which conditions of production almost invariably change), and high overhead costs even after the mill begins to grind. The cycle is roughly as follows: When the price is good the profits are big, and more cane is set out. Little promoters, or those without much reserve cash, start projects which will be foreclosed eventually and fall into stronger hands. This will occur in some period of low prices. A year or two in which the crops are good in more than the average number of the world's cane and beet areas may be the occasion. There are many unpredictable conditions which can take a cent a pound off the price, and even a half-cent would wreck some of these ventures. Instead of production falling off, easing the glut in the market, the supply is likely to increase sharply.

Say the price falls from $3\frac{1}{2}$ cents to $2\frac{1}{2}$ cents a pound in Santo Domingo. Every harassed manager of a sugar *central* will sit up nights figuring out how to pay expenses until better times come. If he improves his machinery, his process or his cane, the result will be more sugar. Almost invariably he will attempt to put more cane through his million-dollar mill in a season in order to reduce the cost per pound. This is perfectly good management, since his great inevitable cost item is the overhead, including the interest charge on a huge capital investment. The same John Doe who is a director in a powerful corporation whose plants are grinding more sugar to cut the production cost per pound, is also a director in a finance syndicate and a machinery company which have mortgages and liens on weaker estates. These creditors foreclose in order to save something. The bigger company takes over the mill which is in trouble, or the bondholders (or perhaps a bank) appoint somebody to manage the plant. In any case, the result is more sugar.

For example, Quisqueya and Las Pajas in Santo Domingo were taken over by the Cuban Dominican group in 1924. Both mills had already been managed for several years by the same interests. Quisqueya had produced about 9,600 short tons in 1914.[2] By 1923, just beyond the great slump in prices, the output had risen by about 4,000 short tons. By 1925, it was 19,000 tons, and the spring estimate for the 1926 crop was 25,000. Boca Chica, managed by its security holders, produced more than twice as much in 1925, during a slump in prices, as in 1923. The grinding season can be arbitrarily shortened or the output cut by collective or government action (as in Cuba in 1926). Unfortunately, sugar is produced in too many parts of the world, under varied conditions and behind different tariff walls, to control the entire output. Theoretically, even the big plants should go bankrupt. They sometimes do, but it is quite as likely that a combination of circumstances will raise the price and start the cycle all over again. World demand, supply and production conditions are all too unstable in sugar to admit of formulating any general economic laws which would be of much use in practice.

While the Cuban Dominican sugar group is not strictly identified with the National City Bank, it is obvious that the relationship has grown stronger since 1920. For example, Mr. Howell has been replaced by a Director of the Bank as President. Those who do not like the National City crowd in Santo Domingo charge that the institution has used its financial power in some cases to collect sugar properties for its stockholders. Two estates, San Marcos and San Carlos, near Puerto Plata, were taken over by the Bank itself, not the related sugar concern. The Chase National Bank also has a small sugar property (Monte Llano), near Puerto Plata. This it acquired as the successor of the American Foreign Banking Corporation, itself the successor of Jarvis's old 1912 *Banco Nacional*. The three greatest sugar groups are the Cuban-Dominican, the Vicini heirs (Italian), and the vast Central Romana in the southeast—a subsidiary of the South Porto Rico Sugar Company. The last began at the time of the 1911-12 revolution. It first shipped cane to the mill at Guanica, Porto Rico, and has always sent some there, where it is ground inside the American tariff wall. The mill at La Romana was set up in 1918 and doubled seven years later by moving machinery from one of the properties in Porto Rico.

A glance at the directorate of the South Porto Rico Sugar Company and the Cuban Dominican suggests that they are quite separate baronies in Sugardom. Mr. Schall, chairman of the South Porto Rico Board of Directors, is President of the American Colonial Bank in San Juan, Porto Rico. Mr. Dillingham, President of the South Porto Rico, is also of the above bank. Mr. Welty, another Director of the sugar concern, is a member of Mr. Schall's firm in New York. Mr. Tilney is of the Bankers Trust Company, and Mr. Horace Havemeyer is also a director of both, besides being a member of Havemeyer & Elder, Inc., and thus a representative of the vague central organization of Sugardom. One director is on the boards of nine different electric power concerns. Two others sit at the director's table of various big insurance companies.

A considerable rivalry exists between the Central Romana (South Porto Rico) and Cuban Dominican groups. For example, the former will not even do business with the National City Bank, but uses the Royal Bank of Canada. Central Romana has stuck pretty exclusively to the sugar business, expanded rapidly but systematically, and made money. There is a certain derision in this group's attitude toward its largest rival, which on its part has related itself in various ways to many kinds of enterprises, and has lost large sums of money in some of its sugar ventures. Barahona, for example, has cost well over $20,000,000—the usual estimate in 1926 was around $24,000,000. It was valued for tax assessment at a shade over $7,000,000 in 1925. On the basis of net earnings since it began grinding, the property would be worth considerably less than nothing. The sugar content of the cane at La Romana is a good 50 percent higher—a decisive factor in the cost of manufacture.

Outside of the Vicini properties and those of the above two American groups, there are five good estates: Sante Fe, Porvenir, Boca, Chica and San Luis. Santa Fe belongs to the Cuban-American Ros family (of New York). Hugh Kelly and Company, of New York, own Porvenir and also the old irrigated Ansonia property near Azua, which is of doubtful value. Besides Hugh Kelly's sons, there is a directorate overlapping somewhat with the Cuban Dominican. Boca Chica is supposedly owned by the Spanish-Dominican Parra Alba and his associates, but managed by a Porto-Rican-American group of bondholders and sugar men. San Luis is nominally the property of Santiago Michelena, formerly a Porto Rican, but now naturalized as a Dominican. This property is heavily mortgaged and was very nearly foreclosed by the National City people in 1924. Michelena took his business to the Bank of Nova Scotia, and gave up his American citizenship in 1925.

The capital investment and acreage devoted to the sugar business in Santo Domingo in 1925 may be indicated by a table. These figures were certified to the writer by the Ministry of Finance. The surface and

SUGAR—INDUSTRIAL FEUDALISM

assessed valuations were those used in computing the property tax, and are generally somewhat low:

THE PRINCIPAL SUGAR ESTATES IN SANTO DOMINGO, 1925

Name	Nationality	Area in Acres***	Value (Assessed)
Consuelo	American	49,354	$5,456,700.43
Barahona	"	49,400	7,130,350.76
Quisqueya	"	8,593	944,603.40
San Isidro	"	20,727	1,500,021.90
Las Pajas	"	5,588	1,243,491.56
San Marcos	"	1,251	120,151.00
San Carlos	"	564	140,355.14
Santa Fe	"	61,069	4,944,025.57
Porvenir	"	10,877	1,644,867.70
Ansonia	"	2,066	422,420.00
Boca Chica	Amer.-P. R.-Domin.****	6,325	527,585.70
Central Romana	American	144,418	9,761,349.07
Monte Llano	"	1,947	389,296.33
Amistad	American-Dominican	3,811	239,921.52
Italia	Italian	8,269	⎫
Azuano	"	4,647	⎬ 1,699,152.90
Ocoa	"	1,941	⎭
Angelina	"	13,317	1,930,640.90
Cristóbal Colón	"	22,175	1,454,660.20
J. J. Serrallés	Italian-Dominican*	12,275	
San Luis	Dominican**	8,346	1,237,697.95
Cuba	"	1,222	106,843.75
	Totals:	438,182	$40,894,135.78

* Old "Porto Rico" mill and estates. No mill now. Furnishes cane to Cristóbal Colón. No valuation in list furnished, and apparently pays no land tax.
** Canadian mortgage and American machinery lien.
*** The Dominican official figures were given in *tareas*: the roughly approximate acreage was obtained by multiplying by .155.
**** This is the mill managed by Porto Rican and American bondholders. The largest stockholder is Parra Alba, a naturalized Dominican of Spanish origin. What, if anything, the stockholders will ever realize is extremely problematical.

Of the total of 438,182 acres, about 125,000 were given by the tax estimate as in cane, 80,000 in pasture, and the rest unused. The Receivership report for 1925 (p. 11) gave the cultivated area as 146,903 acres. Some plantations—notably Consuelo, Central Romana and

San Luis—have greatly increased their acreage since. We shall not be far out of the way in putting the 1926 area in cane at 170,000 acres, the pasture at 100,000 and the unused land at 250,000 acres. About half of this last category is reserve, the other 125,000 acres or so either worn out or never suitable for cane. The Department of Public Works reported 909 kilometers or 565 miles of railway on sugar plantations in 1925. This varied from American-gauge heavy track at La Romana to some very light railway on the Vicini and other properties. Perhaps one-sixth of Santo Domingo's 12,000,000 acres of surface is inhabited—coastal and valley land. Sugar estates own something like a quarter of the best of this.

The Military Government's land registration law of 1920[8] was just what the sugar people had wanted for years. To simplify matters, the order stated that ten years' possession up to January 1, 1921, would give a clear title. American lawyers seized upon a certain vagueness in the language of the American-made law to argue before Dominican courts that the sugar corporations (Central Romana, in the test case) should have credit for any fraction of ten years' possession enjoyed before the above date. That is, if the land had already been held three years, the concern argued the right to prove up January 1, 1928, etc. This was still in the courts in 1926 when the writer left Santo Domingo.

A huge, heavily capitalized and mainly foreign owned export industry of this kind, thrust in the midst of a relatively primitive country, has far-reaching economic effects. Thousands of acres of timber are often ruthlessly destroyed in getting a plantation started. In the early days of the American Receivership, about half the value of Santo Domingo's exports was supplied by raw sugar. Later a molasses trust appeared, and this commodity reached a value of $731,057 in 1925. Sugar, sugar cane and molasses to the value of $16,868,734, or 63 percent of the total exports, were sent out in that year. Thus one crop created nearly two-thirds of the purchasing power abroad. This was produced almost wholly with foreign capital. On the one hand, the well-paid directive and technical personnel was largely foreign; on the other hand, thousands of Haitians and British West India blacks were imported to perform the common labor at low wages.

Some taxes—especially local ones—are paid by the sugar concerns. Corrupt and incompetent municipal governments are an almost inevitable result. At La Romana and Barahona large sums of money have left little trace in the way of public improvements. Native business is almost paralyzed in many such localities by the presence of company stores.

Where does this $16,000,000 or so a year, the price of exported sugar, go? Some is collected abroad as interest, dividends, payments on machinery, etc. If we say that the machinery is brought to Santo Domingo, the fact remains that it is used there to mine more soil fertility and export it in the form of sugar. Some is paid in Santo Domingo as salaries and wages, but these also go largely to foreigners. The basic wage for day labor in 1926 was 60 cents a day.

Much has been written about Santo Domingo's "favorable balance of trade," which has sometimes run into many millions of dollars. All this means is that the value of these exports never came back at all. Just how this is "favorable" to Santo Domingo it is a little hard to see.

On the assumption that agriculture was thereby "improved" and "modernized," the heavy implements used by the sugar concerns were put on the free list by the Military Government. As far as an outsider can see, the main effect of this was to favor sugar at the expense of the diversified agriculture which natives could carry on without such machinery. Santo Domingo imports over two million dollars' worth a year of grains and fruits. Famous for her cattle, she buys abroad over a half-million pairs of boots, shoes and slippers annually, and more than a million dollars' worth of meat. Over two million pounds of fresh potatoes were imported in 1925. During that same year, this country, with mile upon mile of forests, bought over a half million dollars' worth of wood and wood products.

Though the United States had an overwhelming superiority in this nearby export market, Dominican sugar goes elsewhere on account of our tariff. After the rates of 1921 went into effect, our takings dropped unevenly from 70 percent for that year to barely more than 2 percent in 1925. The United Kingdom, Canada, Holland and France were the big purchasers. This situation was made the occasion for the "Law 190" group of taxes against our produce in 1925. At bottom, these laws represented an attempt to correct the Military Government's tariff "reforms," which Dr. Peynado had complained of as granting America everything without giving Santo Domingo anything in exchange.

Cane sugar, as cultivated at present, is the curse of the West Indies. In Santo Domingo, it leads to the foreign ownership of huge tracts of the best land, cultivated largely with annually imported cheap labor. Sugar has not paid in Haiti merely because peasant proprietorship has resisted all attempts to break it up or make it produce one crop on contract. Overpopulated

SUGAR—INDUSTRIAL FEUDALISM

Porto Rico is largely owned by big American sugar, tobacco and citrus fruit companies. Sugar is a double curse there and in Cuba because of "advantages" under the American tariff which put unsuitable land under the one crop and discourage diversified farming.

Some of the finest people alive are in this business. Most of the Americans do not mistreat their labor. The complaints on this score in Santo Domingo have been directed mainly against the Italian estates. The trouble is economic, and it is fundamental. It is dangerous for efficient foreigners to own so much of the soil. Their privilege of importing cheap labor is vicious, but apparently necessary if the present amount of sugar is to be grown. A great deal of land in the West Indies has been worn out and left overpopulated by similar methods in the past. No country can afford it.

The consumer might have to pay more by having his sugar grown under standards of living comparable to his own and conditions of cultivation which would not render the ground sterile for future generations. If in order to achieve this it is necessary to limit ourselves to beet sugar, produced where we can watch it done, perhaps even that price would not be too much to pay. Long ago we began doing something to ease our consciences about people who toiled for us in factories. Sooner or later in this shrinking world we have got to face the same question of exploiting the poorly paid and ignorant a little farther away. If it is really necessary to aid the peoples of these warmer countries in meeting present-day conditions and achieving the best which science makes possible, there ought to be some better way of doing it than turning loose a lot of private corporations to make all the money they can for their stockholders.

CHAPTER XIII

ECONOMIC PENETRATION

Men do otherwise than they intend.—BOSSUET

AFTER the foundering of the San Domingo Improvement Company's *Banque Nationale* just at the opening of the present century, banking operations were carried on by merchants for some years. Santiago Michelena, a Porto Rican, was one of the occasional honest men among these merchant bankers. Besides, he was an American citizen. When Dawson and Dillingham were trying to get the first customs receivership going early in 1905, Michelena aided them by acting as a sort of unofficial receiver. When the modus vivendi was finally set up in April of that year, he was made the depositary of its funds.

The first of the great foreign private banks to install itself in Santo Domingo was the Royal Bank of Canada, which came in 1908. It is still the second largest in the Republic. Santo Domingo has never regulated this bank's activities much. Since it is evidently solvent, and does not issue currency, why should she? Most of the insurance business has always been British. The Royal Bank of Canada has had its share of the sugar business —even with some of the largest American firms. There are savings accounts and remittances for the British West India personnel employed around the sugar estates. Nowadays, Canada and the British Isles take most of the Dominican sugar, and there is of course other British

ECONOMIC PENETRATION

commerce in both directions. The bank has money to lend on mortgages, etc., and does a conservative general business. It had some accounts tied up and even a number of losses in the debacle following 1920, but nothing to compare with those of its largest rival, the International Banking Corporation.

Next after the Royal Bank of Canada came the Jarvis *Banco Nacional* of 1912. It was likewise tempted by the high interest rates—often 12 percent—with security which seemed ample with plenty of watching on the spot. For a time, early in the Bryan-Sullivan regime, it held the Receivership account. This was—and is—a very tempting plum. If the recipient is strong and shrewd enough to handle it, he can hold Dominican money at a low American rate of interest and keep much out at high Dominican rates, besides collecting fees for transmitting sums which can be canceled off with commercial payments and thus never moved at all. Jarvis was unable to keep this account, which went back to Michelena.

The National City Bank subsidiary, the International Banking Corporation, bought out Michelena in the spring of 1917. Through interlocking directorates, this group was more involved in the sugar business than either of its rivals on the ground. Its vast resources and its head office in New York were a great convenience in those war days, especially as the Military Government was establishing a purchasing agency in that city. At that time, when world tonnage was pretty well tied up, the United States had something approaching a monopoly in the Dominican import trade, as well as taking most of the exports.

By the time the post-war sugar inflation—commonly known in the West Indies as the "dance of the millions"

—was at its height, one of the above three banks had disappeared and two others had arrived. During 1920, the *Banco Nacional* sold out to the American Foreign Banking Corporation of New York. This concern was owned by a group of national banks, the President of its Board of Trustees holding the same position in the Chase National Bank of New York. The other Bank was the *Banco Territorial y Agricola* of San Juan, Porto Rico. The American Foreign Banking Corporation was one of the casualties of the liquidation period, and the Chase National Bank finally took over its assets in 1926. This concern does no banking business in the Republic. On the first of January of that same year, the National City Bank replaced its affiliated concern, which meant chiefly a change in bookkeeping. The Bank of Nova Scotia arrived just after the "dance of the millions," and thus had no bad debts to collect. In 1926, therefore, the four great foreign banks were the Royal Bank of Canada, the National City Bank, the Bank of Nova Scotia and the *Banco Territorial y Agricola,* two American and two British. There are some native concerns, but they are not important relative to the foreign ones.

It is unnecessary to more than mention several reasons why the National City group is criticized in Santo Domingo with a harshness which the others are spared. The American Military Government brought it in. Its foreign sugar connections would not endear it to the Dominicans in any case; especially as it has been mixed in the taking over, under financial pressure, of a number of the native-owned estates. One or two other cases were felt to have involved ruthlessness, but that of Michelena, who escaped the foreclosure, is commonly regarded as conclusive. That he was not actually insolvent seemed to be demonstrated by the fact that a conservative British bank was willing to assume the risk. Moreover there was a question of ingratitude. Did not the American group owe its whole position in the Republic to the work of this man?

Perhaps the foreclosures were defensible. I am merely repeating the explanations given by intelligent—and, to be sure, sometimes interested—people concerning a general feeling of suspicion, fear and dislike. As one prominent American business man, not himself a banker, put it: "A bank is a bank. It is supposed to stick to banking, not to go around trying to separate people from their property in the interest of its henchmen." The other side of it is that Americans were not the only performers in the "dance of the millions." Many people felt, however, that American money had been pressed upon them at the peak of the boom. Under these circumstances, a bank can make a lot of enemies in a small country by trying rather persistently to collect thirteen or fourteen millions of dollars in hard times.

Dominican law allows a proved consignee to take goods from the custom-house with a mere copy of the bill of lading, instead of being obliged to get the original at a bank by making settlement. As a result, many shippers have brought pressure upon the National City Bank to act as consignee. A considerable business of this kind has grown up, which the bank did not want and did not feel itself adequately equipped to handle. The role is rather a necessary one, but not popular.

Finally, this bank, both as Government depository and as the one great New York institution, naturally plays a leading part in adjusting a balance of payments with the United States which is irritating as well as trying to the Dominicans. After the war, we were no longer important takers of their tobacco. Since 1921, we have gradually ceased to furnish a market for their sugar. Santo Domingo ordinarily has a large export balance in her total trade, but the opposite is now the case in the commerce with the United States alone. This excess of imports was over $3,000,000 in 1922 and 1923, over $5,000,000 in 1924 and double that in 1925. Resentment against our tariff came to a climax during that year in the "Law 190" group of taxes.

In making a supposed most-favored-nation agreement with Santo Domingo in September 1924, the American Government actually reserved the important items: our very special treatment of Cuban sugar, and the whole question of commerce with or between our "territories or possessions," including the Canal Zone. Santo Domingo is more than three times closer even to our northern port of New York than to Liverpool or Havre. She is wedged in between American Porto Rico and the Virgin Islands on the East and our protectorate in Haiti on the West, with favored Cuba and our southern States beyond. As a result, she is economically a victim of propinquity, apparently doomed not to rule even in her own house. The American reservations in 1924 meant that trade was not to be reasonably free along the arc of the West Indies, from Florida to South America. All the passenger services except that of the Clyde Line to New York and the weekly boat of the Bull Insular Line to Porto Rico, are irregular. The Clyde ships are old, small, slow and uncomfortable. To go by the Bull Insular Line to San Juan and thence to New York also takes a good deal of time, and is expensive.

With freight it is much the same. The Clyde and Bull Insular vessels, both American, furnish the only frequent regular services. French and Dutch ships make occasional stops. There are three East and West lines, from Cuban or Gulf ports, none of them very good. Practically all the rest of the service is sporadic and often seasonal. We take what we want, which happens to be the import trade into Santo Domingo. Naturally our percentage fell off somewhat when we practically quit importing two of the four main products, sugar and tobacco. Between 1921 and 1925, our share of Dominican imports fell from 83.97 percent to 65.12 percent; but in the same period we dropped from 77.7 percent of the exports to 20.95 percent! The nature of the imports can be best shown by a condensed table:[1]

AMERICAN PREDOMINANCE IN
SANTO DOMINGO'S IMPORTS, 1925

Article	From U. S.	Total Imported
Agricultural machinery	$93,957	$216,755
Cars, carriages	1,349,961	1,385,019
Chemical and pharmaceutical products	418,674	626,260
Coal, coke, briquets	76,325	77,837
Copper and alloys	128,126	144,006
Cotton, and manufactures of	3,305,496	4,485,611
Earthenware, porcelain	72,435	202,796
Fiber, vegetable	495,574	1,168,869
Foodstuffs:		
Meats	1,042,015	1,202,076
Fish	376,188	442,623
Grains, fruits	1,485,330	3,368,922
Liquors and beverages	34,217	580,136
Canned or preserved goods	113,161	166,729
Miscellaneous	552,539	1,088,288

Article	From U. S.	Total Imported
Glass and glassware	$84,097	$153,130
Hats and caps	65,083	175,622
Hides and skins	826,086	1,177,446
Iron and steel:		
Cast iron	21,960	58,388
Wrought iron	1,289,364	1,677,571
Machinery and apparatus	1,488,365	1,664,307
Oils, mineral	699,739	1,536,783
Paints and pigments	134,393	185,050
Paper and manufactures	286,582	457,387
Perfumery and cosmetics	45,519	129,353
Rubber	324,689	362,526
Silk	315,242	482,932
Soap	273,007	366,097
Woods	577,009	638,412
Wools	97,985	243,092

The part played by American banks in an economic penetration which, as we shall see, only begins with sugar and shipping, has been greatly overestimated. If the National City Bank and the *Banco Territorial y Agricola* should leave, the two great Canadian institution would serve similar commercial and industrial interests in about the same way. For a long period, the most important foreign sugar group was the Italian, yet there never was an Italian bank of any importance in the Republic. There was no bank at all of any size for years before the Royal Bank of Canada opened in 1908. The sugar business grew as fast up to 1917, when the National City group arrived, as it did afterwards.

None of these branches of great foreign banks make public the amount of capital they employ in Santo

Domingo, the turnover of their business or its exact nature. Their great strength lies in the fact that they do not need any definitely assigned capital for one small country. Dominicans do business with them because they seem strong and safe. If the world ever becomes internationally organized, it will be possible to bring about more publicity concerning these matters, perhaps to establish some general principles of banking legislation in which weak countries will be supported, and to cure certain abuses.

Foreign lumber companies claim far more surface than the sugar companies hold. Santo Domingo has the largest remaining supply of good mahogany in the world. In 1926 an American concern, the Orme Mahogany Company, announced that it held a concession of about a half million acres.[2] N. L. Orme, the President, is listed in the 1925 report of the American Customs Receivership as "special Inspector, Macoris." Señor Lopez was apparently unaware of this connection, but charged that other officers of the Mahogany Company were employed by the Receivership.

There is an Enriquillo Company which claims between 400,000 and 500,000 acres in the southwestern part of the Republic. In its early prospectuses, it mentioned Santo Domingo as an American "protectorate," which it never has been. A prospective stockholder wrote the Chamber of Commerce at Washington, which took up the question of the concession, as usual, with the American Consulate. If this were always done by investors, many losses would be averted. We have had honest and capable men in the Consulate at Santo Domingo City for years. Suffice it to say that the Chamber of Commerce did not get a very favorable report on this venture. Later, some of the solider stockholders reorganized the company with J. H. Edwards, former Deputy Receiver, as President. Attempts have since been made to develop the tract, some of which is across the boundary claimed by Haiti. Much of the land has not been surveyed and is subject to *peso* or share titles. Sisal, rubber, cotton and sugar are among the possibilities, besides the valuable timber.

The Habanero Lumber Company has vast holdings, some also under vague titles, mainly in the province of Azua. The figure in *tareas* given the writer at the Santo Domingo office would make about a half million acres. This concern is a subsidiary of the Gulf Red Cedar Company and the Richmond Cedar Works, and they are in turn held by the American and Eagle Pencil Companies. Nominally, their interest is in pencil cedar. In practice, lumbering must be done systematically in order to pay, selling the woods not wanted by the concessionaires for their own use.

The Barahona Wood Products Company managed by a former employee of the Military Government, turns out caster wheels for furniture from *lignum vitae*. This concern is a subsidiary of the Bassick Company, itself controlled by the Bassick-Alemite Corporation, which is held by the Stewart-Warner Speedometer Corporation. Only the bigger logs of lignum vitae are valuable enough to export for propeller bushing in steamships, for bowling balls, etc. Quite small pieces, including waste, can be worked up into caster wheels on the ground. There was a fierce controversy in 1926 about the use of this small timber, the claim being made that it devastated the forests.[3]

Many Americans have gone broke trying to raise cotton in Santo Domingo, notably the long-staple varieties. As in Haiti, the pests have proved too active.

There is a "tree-cotton" in Haiti which does very well in native hands, producing smaller crops regularly with little attention. This does not interest the foreigner, who wants to use large-scale methods and make a great deal of money immediately. If cotton, sisal and rubber should ever became solidly established, they might very well give the final *coup de grace* to Dominican economic independence.

There is a great deal of potential grain country in the upland valleys of Santo Domingo. H. P. Krippene's little (American) flour mill at Puerto Plata has rested since its beginning, in 1923, upon the hope that it would stimulate the cultivation of high-grade wheat. So far, it has imported its wheat from the United States and Canada, duty free. Thus is competition with imported flour made possible, as this pays a duty. Every time there is agitation for a tariff on wheat, this miller bustles around, distributing seed and so on, as though he really meant to promote the crop in Santo Domingo. Then the political squall blows over and the mill goes on collecting a living by grinding tax-free wheat into "domestic" flour to compete with the dutiable foreign brands. This miller is not the diplomat that he may seem from the above. He refuses to deal with the National City Bank, which holds the paper of many, many merchants, and could throw orders his way. Business, like politics, is well tinctured with "the seeming things that cunning times put on." He had better look out, or he may find himself in unequal conflict with the Bank.

Machinery is one of the pivots of economic Americanization. In a rich little country with only about twenty people to the square mile, it seems obvious that life could be made easier if only there were iron arms to lift the burdens. Rarely does it occur to the American enthusiast that after the mechanization the population would be less sparse, and there would be more burdens to lift. The Dominican does not envy the landless Porto Rican. On the contrary Porto Rico is held up as the horrible example of what Santo Domingo does not want to become.

In the Ms. copy of the 1923 annual Consular Report appeared a suggestive discussion of American machinery. Santo Domingo ranked twenty-third in the world's markets for these exports. She took twice as much of our machinery as did Rumania, and more than Germany, Sweden or the Dutch East Indies. America had been furnishing from 84 to 99.9 percent. Between 1910 and 1921, this item in the trade between the two countries ranged from $254,995 to $3,252,954. The biggest year, 1921, was abnormal, as many sugar mills begun in the boom period were then being completed. Pre-eminence was given American machines both by the presence of our sugar people and by the long tenure of American engineers in the Public Works services. Some sugar mills furnish electric light and power to nearby towns, equipped, of course, with American fixtures.

American automobiles, motor trucks and tractors have practically a complete monopoly of the market. The Ford naturally comes first in a country where macadam roads often give way to trails, containing rocks and stumps or running for miles along the dry, gravelly beds of streams. Various products of the General Motors Company are strongly represented. Among the higher priced cars, there are a good many Packards and even some Lincolns. Light and medium-weight trucks are the commonest, but there are also some very

ECONOMIC PENETRATION

heavy ones which cut up the asphalt roads near the larger cities.

Perhaps the best index of the growth of motor transport is the importation of gasoline. The figure for 1917 was 1,488,009 litres, valued at $117,450. In 1920, $430,278 was paid for 4,113,596 litres. Imports increased 50 percent in quantity by 1923, but the price had dropped so that the cost was only about $50,000 more. By 1925 the imports had risen to 10,642,311 litres, costing $797,192. Of this huge quantity, 8,465,-249 litres came from the United States and Porto Rico, the remaining 2,177,062 from the Dutch West Indies.[4]

Thus the consumption rose seven-fold between 1917 and 1925, to a value of nearly $800,000. Of this the American share was roughly 76 percent and the British 24. The Royal Dutch Shell combination, predominantly British, gets its oil from the Dutch West Indies. Oil has often been reported in Santo Domingo, but never tapped in paying quantities. An Interocean Oil Company held a concession under the Military Government to drill in the province of Azua. Operations had ceased and most of the machinery had been exported by 1925. The American Consulate reported a rumor in August of that year that "The West Indies Petroleum Company, Ltd." had acquired the concession, but the writer could find out nothing about a probable resumption at the time of his visit in 1926. There is oil visible in places on top of the ground, but the process of separating it would be too expensive at present prices.

Two American companies have (1926) main organizations in the capital, with various branches: the West India Oil Company (Standard) and the Texas Company. The former arrived in 1909, the latter in 1916.

Tide Water Oil is handled by a Porto Rican firm; the Sun Oil Company's Products by the Santo Domingo Motors Company (American-Italian). The Sinclair Oil Company is represented by an Italian Dominican group, Ferreccio, Vicini y Cia. The heaviest competitor of the two American companies first mentioned is the Imperial Oil Company (British—the Royal Dutch-Shell combination). It has an agency in the capital and a sub-agency at Macoris. The Americans have accused the Shell people of "unfair tactics," such as giving away pumps. In a few months this British group climbed from insignificance to about a fifth of the gasoline business.

Motor transport is gradually choking the Scotch railway which runs eastward to Sanchez on Samana Bay. It costs about 52 cents a quintal to haul cacao from the La Vega region in the Royal Plain to the steamer at Sanchez by rail. Where the turnpikes are completed, a motor truck can lay it on the dock alongside the steamer in Santo Domingo City for about 35 cents. The railway is probably doomed when the highway system gets nearer completion. Very likely, the line from Puerto Plata to Santiago, which has very bad grades, will be in a similar position with the completion of the road already well under way. It seems to the writer unfortunate that the railway roadbed was not used for the road, at a great saving of expense. This was done at Gonaives, Haiti. An over-steep railway grade may be perfectly good for a road.

There are some hydro-electric power sites in Santo Domingo, but these seem likely to fall into foreign hands as fast as development becomes feasible. One at Jimenoa Falls, southeast of La Vega, was surveyed and reported capable of furnishing 9,000 horsepower. In June, 1925, one Dr. Villalon and Mr. Frank Steinhart, the electric

·light and power magnate of Havana, went to New York to interest other "American bankers and capitalists" in developing a concession from the Dominican Government. Steinhart is connected with Speyer and Company of New York. The status of this project in 1926 seemed to be that the promoters and the Government were waiting for each other to do something about building the necessary road.[5]

A mass of small ventures, such as the dye-extracting plant at Monte Cristi, may be passed over. All of these foreign enterprises make their money out of the same general economic and social situation. There are some special products, such as dyewoods and lignum vitae, but the main factors are cheap labor and cheap land. Good cane land costs from about a sixth to a third of the Louisiana price. Where labor is hired by the day, which is not often done, the rate is usually sixty cents.

Reliable figures of average earnings at piece work such as cane-cutting are impossible to get. One of the Vicini foremen guessed eighty cents. While this may be a fair estimate for the one property, the writer checked it a number of times and thinks it above the average for unskilled labor on these Italian properties. There was so much complaint of bad treatment on the Angelina estate during the 1924-25 season that the British established an office in Saint Kitts with the avowed purpose of boycotting employers who failed to "treat the men humanely."[6] My own opinion, founded on a good many observations, estimates and comparisons, is that unskilled earnings at piece work may average as high as 90 cents a day at La Romana, but not over 80 for the whole Republic. This is a third higher than the basic rate by the day, but some allowance must be made for the seasonal and temporary character of the work.

A Haitian day-laborer at home is paid 30 American cents by the Public Works Department, and 20 to 30 outside. The writer is positive, after surveys in both countries, that the Haitian profits by his seasonal move but that his presence has a bad effect on wage levels in Santo Domingo. Comparisons are difficult, as the cost and standards of living are higher in Porto Rico and Cuba, and lower in Haiti, than in Santo Domingo. Official sanitary reports show 70 percent or more of the population of Haiti to be suffering from venereal disease. Malaria is rife, and there are both amoebic and bacillic dysenteries, not to mention cases of leprosy and elephantiasis (filaria).

Whether health conditions are any better in Santo Domingo has been a subject of controversy. At any rate the Dominicans would be glad[7] to dispense with their 100,000 or so of annual Haitian visitors. This alien and undesired element is about a tenth of the population of the country. The American Minister compared these people favorably with the Dominicans as workers, doubted if they were more diseased, and remarked that they were necessary during the sugar season. Minister Russell's departure was an occasion of quiet but sincere rejoicing. Not only did his part in establishing the Military Government bring up tormented memories, but his years of residence had failed to bring him into sympathy with the Dominican point of view. His successor, Mr. Young, is happily of a different temperament and caliber. Both peoples might have been spared a good deal if we had kept first-rate men in this difficult post from the start.

Cheap imported seasonal labor digs a pit of subsistance wages at the feet of the Dominican worker in the interest of the sugar business. There is little for him to climb to when the leading industry of his country also imports its highly paid directive and technical personnel. Because it preempts so much of the richest and best situated land, he is hampered in turning to the soil. It takes the cream of the mercantile business in many localities. A few good Dominican lawyers like the Peynados manage to make a living, but foreign business pays its fees mainly to imported ones. To be a first-rate doctor, the native must have enough money to study abroad. There is no coal, oil or iron on which to found manufactories, even if a high American and a low Dominican tariff—both made by Americans—did not render it well nigh impossible to get a start. A Dominican can move between nearby ports with a sailboat, but the real traffic is sewn up in a bag by the big foreign companies. He may start a jitney business in or between towns, buying his foreign-made flivver from a foreign agent.

What little unionism exists in Santo Domingo has the reputation of being radical. The marvel is that labor can maintain any organization at all in a country which uses tens of thousands of foreign workers who could get a maximum of thirty cents a day at home. These Haitians speak a dialect made up of a few hundred words originally French, but now oftentimes unrecognizable as such, and a grammar simplified beyond belief. They are picturesque enough, but so are Chinese coolies. This annual invasion, much of which evades the law and remains, brings along its women, its voodoo drums with their sacred tufts of goats' hair, and its *wanga* or magic of horses' skulls, toasted corn, pig-fat, and no white man knows what-all. Aside from a small "élite" which gets its culture direct from France and remains apart, Haiti is African. Santo Domingo may be more or less corrupt Spanish, but she is Spanish nevertheless. All the voodooism in the country is freshly imported. There is no sharply drawn color line, but the disagreeable elements of one are forced on the country by a seasonal labor problem for which foreign economic penetration is solely responsible.

The Dominican merchant loses a large part of the cream of the trade because it consists of foreigners importing for themselves or selling to each other. On the other hand the workers he sells to are poorer because of the importation of cheap Haitians. The factories are so far away, and the haul so expensive, that the return of goods is practically out of the question. Merchants must keep small stocks or sustain heavy losses on unsalable goods. A number of foreign consuls, interviewed by the writer, generally agreed on the point that their home people must be advised to send cheap goods, intended to sell at a large margin of profit, and with a slow turnover in mind.

High prices, sluggish turnover and inadequate stocks are exactly the kind of competition the foreign mail-order house wants in order to gather a harvest of orders. The result is congested customs houses, as well as an outcry from the retailers. There is no specific remedy for this situation, which arises from the general disease of economic dependency. As long as sugar remains a sort of state within the state—with its own exporting, importing, retailing, transportation, repairs, and even labor—it will smother every other line of business which does not obediently dovetail in and take what is left.

CHAPTER XIV

IS THERE A "YANKEE PERIL"?

No fundamental study of Latin-American problems has yet been made by any branch of our government. We have dealt so far only with manners, the amenities of life, and the opportunities to do a profitable business.—Isaiah Bowman.

There have been innumerable allusions in Santo Domingo to "Yankee Imperialism" and the "Yankee Peril." Widely circulated works by outsiders have referred to the country as a "protectorate," a "virtual protectorate," an "actual protectorate," "practically an American protectorate," a "financial protectorate" and so on. The charge of "economic imperialism" has often been lodged, usually without any attempt at exact definition.

All these terms can be misleading if carelessly applied to the territorial expansion of the United States or the business of Americans abroad. One writer after another has borrowed a terminology which grew up around the penetration of Africa and Asia by rival European states. Very general treatises, where many enterprises are skeletonized with almost no detail, have a way of omitting some vital distinctions. Especially in the numerous books which deal mainly with the Old World but add a few incidental pages or chapters on the New, are the mechanisms artificially forced into the same mould. In dealing with only one country, we can be a little more definite.

Santo Domingo is not a protectorate in the correct sense of the term, and never has been. Morocco, under French "protection" since 1912, is a very good example of this type of control. France has a treaty right to carry on Moroccan foreign relations. To attack the Sultan is to attack France, and to insult him is to insult her foreign service. This first earmark of an Old World protectorate is always missing in the New, because there is only one strong power over her, which maintains a policy known as the Monroe Doctrine. European states have a blanket warning against interfering directly with the affairs of any American nation. No treaty is necessary.

The next earmark of a protectorate is an important amount of control over *internal* affairs, administration and oftentimes justice to some degree, as distinguished from *external* relations. Supervision over finances, arms and armed forces are the two main items. France has control over all in Morocco. So have the Americans in Haiti, which is often mentioned in official documents as a protectorate. Haiti has another of the characteristics in that a native government has been preserved continuously, together with the fiction of "sovereignty." We have very little to do with justice there. While we maintain a pretty rigid control over finances, including both collections and expenditures, the treaties are definitely time-limited by their terms. This is not true of European protectorates. France has a very definite official colonization policy in both Morocco and Tunis, openly founded on the idea of permanency. We may let Haiti pass as a protectorate, but one of a highly modified type. Especially does the assumption that it is definitely time-limited distinguish it from those of the Old World. Associated with this is the fact that American policy has

IS THERE A "YANKEE PERIL"?

never envisaged the use of the armed forces of protected states for our own ends. After a considerable sojourn in European protectorates the writer is prepared to assert that this last distinction is fundamental. The practical differences between the two sets of imperial problems in the Old and New Worlds are even more striking than the more theoretical, legal ones, but we have no space for them here.

Our customs receivership in Santo Domingo, as officially established by the 1907 Convention, did not constitute even a "financial protectorate." The State Department tried to convert it into one between 1914 and 1916 by putting the remainder of the revenues under the American collection service and installing a "financial expert" who would have had large powers in the other half of the field: disbursements. When the Dominican Government blocked this move, a military dictatorship was set up. This lasted from the fall of 1916 to the fall of 1922, with some vestiges of it for two years longer.

Santo Domingo is not a protectorate under the evacuation treaty of 1924. The 1907 customs receivership continued in force. If the new convention designed to replace that of 1907 should become fully effective, the life of this collection service would be lengthened, but the power of the receivership over Dominican finances is very much less than it was in 1916. The explanation of this is in the realm of facts rather than that of legal theories. Before the days of the Military Government, the internal revenues were insignificant, the budget being covered almost entirely by the customs receipts which passed through American hands. Aside from loans, the gross receipts of the Republics in 1925 were $11,645,931.69. Of this only $4,836,560.71 came through the American Receivership.[1] The rest was collected by the Dominican Treasury in the form of internal revenue, various general and special receipts, including the national lottery, and as income from the Government railway. From a practical monopoly of collections in the earlier days of the Receivership, we were down to a little over 40 percent in 1925.

No nation is eternal. We can only guess what the political alignment of the world will be even after a few hundred years. As far as the eye can penetrate into the future, however, it is certain that Santo Domingo will continue to be of special naval concern to the United States because of its position before the gates of Panama and the Gulf of Mexico. Whether or not the Monroe Doctrine itself is a manifestation of imperialism is a point which need not be labored. Since the evacuation in 1924, the Dominicans have not lived in any imminent fear of political engulfment. This easier tendency in affairs may be temporary. The future is impenetrable in that respect, "all the old prophets being dead and all the young ones liars."

There is, nevertheless, a real "Yankee peril" in Santo Domingo. The more dramatic elements of politics, diplomacy and military adventures have often tended to obscure the relentless march of economic forces. It has seemed convenient in the preceding chapters to deal with this creeping parasitism of foreign business under three main heads: (1) The land question, with sugar and timber the most important products so far; (2) The technique of foreign marketing which, aided by propinquity and tariffs, has held for us practically the same degree of commercial supremacy we enjoyed when Santo Domingo was more primitive; (3) The growth of

American foreign banking as an adjunct to our commercial and industrial enterprises abroad.

Some of the atmosphere of fraud and chicanery which surrounded public loans to unstable governments fifty years ago has been dissipated. People like Edward Hartmont would not find it so easy in this age of classified financial information to list their fraudulent paper on great stock exchanges and mulct both the small European investor and the coming generations in weak states. If America plays a larger part in foreign loans today, it is because her wealth has grown, relative to that of the rest of the world. American commercial banking abroad has become much more powerful, and dangerous, since our inferiority in this respect was recognized and cures sought in the Federal Reserve Act of 1913.

We would be merely shielding our eyes from the greatest "Yankee peril" if we sought it in governmental plots against the independence of Latin-American countries. The menace consists rather of the unpremeditated effects of our commercial efficiency, backed by highly organized and generally well-intentioned government services, which are nevertheless often blind to the consequences of what they promote. Whether or not this is "economic imperialism," it is none the less dangerous for being largely unconscious. Efficiency is congenitally blind to the distant future because its vision is intensely focussed on something else.

We must get rid of our pre-war way of looking at things. During the twelve years following 1913, our exports increased by more than a third, Germany's declined almost as much, and Great Britain's suffered somewhat less. In brief, we occupy a far more important place in the world market than we did. Latin-America finds our commercial invasion more disquieting than she did that of Europe, not only because of our nearness, but due also to our peculiar organization for production. Our vast territory is extremely rich in industrial raw materials. We are unhampered by overpopulation, by the exhausting European competition for man-power, and by the multiplicity of tariff subdivisions which break Europe's home markets up into small compartments and destroy the foundations of mass production.

With cheap fuel and iron, plentiful land, a relatively sparse population and high-priced labor, we have achieved a standard of living which gives us an unprecedented home market. This market lays the foundation for mass production by machinery. On this foundation, we can turn out standardized products at prices which nobody else can duplicate.

This economic colossus, whose domination of the West Indies is becoming intolerable, has one fatal weakness away from home unless armed force is resorted to. That weakness arises from the American standard of living itself. Let the *Yanqui* acquire land and he will set it in sugar cane, exploit it with his expensive machines, hire natives to do the dirty work, and generally take charge. Keep him from owning land and nine-tenths of his economic power disappears. The Spanish commercial salesman has triumphed in Cuba because he can live cheaper. The tobacco trust has never been able entirely to get rid of the small producer who lives frugally and uses so little capital as to be immune from attack on that score. Other West Indian peoples are beginning to study Cuba for clues as to what to avoid. They see eighty-five percent of the machine industry of sugar in American hands. This carries with it control of a huge agricultural industry which, fostered by special tariff privileges in the United States, has choked off other crops and left the island an economic vassal. The pivotal question is land ownership.

There is still plenty of land in Santo Domingo, as good as any in use. It can be reached by building roads. That is, if the spread of foreign proprietorship can be checked in the near future, the country can be saved from the fate of Porto Rico, and a native can have a little plot of his own. There is a movement in Santo Domingo, still in its promising infancy, to check this particular foreign menace by law. It is possible, of course, that the American Government will rise in its benevolent wrath and prevent this solution with threats of force. If that should occur, we need not be embarrassed as to what term to employ—an economic penetration consciously backed by the public force of the State is undoubtedly imperialism.

Barring such a resort to crude economic imperialism, the Dominican Government can gradually bring the foreign latifundia under control. It is necessary to lean over backward at the outset in the encouragement of those crops and industries which will enable the native to own his farm and to work it without too much capital. Sugar would never have gotten the start it has without very special favors, such as tax exemptions, on the assumption that it would be good for the country. There is no point to making tax concessions on the kinds of agricultural implements mainly used by foreign corporations, unless these latter are wanted.

Laws 190 and 278 are well conceived in principle, but they pay too much attention to revenue. A taxation system may be used within limits to shape economic life. Santo Domingo might very well get most of her revenues by taxing things which need to be discouraged. The unnecessary number of pleasure automobiles is one of the little vices which could be made to pay more, taking some of the burden off of gasoline, which is also used in essential transport services. Economic vassalage comes from the excessive consumption of imported goods quite as much as it does from weaknesses in production. If the Military Government went too far in imposing the property tax, the Dominicans have also made a mistake in letting it decay so completely. There is no reason, however, why the foreign corporation, which lives by exporting the country's fertility, should not pay more than the native. This feature of the sugar business must be regulated sooner or later. The companies cannot go on indefinitely, exhausting one area and clearing another, with no thought of soil conservation.

The walls of secrecy which surround international economic relations are due less to conspiracy than to certain curious facts about the complication of modern business, including government business, and the details of organization. That the supposedly annual volumes of *Foreign Relations* have fallen a decade behind time has been partially due to a desire to let things cool, but also to technical difficulties of editing and publication. The effect has been lamentable, nevertheless. What timely information the public gets is largely through press releases, handed out in mimeographed form. A treaty or convention is a mere shred of a long historical process. It must be accompanied by some introductory and explanatory matter in order to be utilizable by reporters or editorial writers. With the best intentions in the world, these lucid expositions are excuses, prepared by the same Department of State which is responsible for the act or document explained. It is the fluent analysis

IS THERE A "YANKEE PERIL"?

rather than the technical document which the gentlemen of the press find it easiest to work from. The mimeographed statement headed, like most of them, simply "To the Press," dated December 24, 1920, was an extreme case. It did not give the correspondence, but consisted of a suave apology for the Government's Dominican policy from the beginning together with a statement of the proposed next move.

Even in branches of the Government service, the left hand does not always know what the right is doing. Our Customs Receiver in Santo Domingo makes annual reports which are public documents. To him the $20,000,000 loan of 1908, with interest at 5 percent, was simply a fact. That it did not sell at par or yield $20,000,000, and really cost the Dominicans 5½ percent on what it did bring, was none of his business—that was past. This loan had another grave fault which the public had no way of seeing or suspecting. Santo Domingo took up a fraction of these bonds every year. They went into a sinking fund where they continued to pay interest. This interest had to come out of the Dominican revenues, even in years when they were insufficient. Whenever such a loan is finally extinguished, this occurs all at once. One day the public revenue is loaded with a payment at the minimum rate of $1,200,000 a year; the next the burden is gone. To find itself suddenly enriched is a severe enough shock to a wealthy and highly stable government.

After the National City Bank loan of 1913 was contracted, Santo Domingo was paying off debt at such a rate that she was always in difficulties to meet current expenses. This situation was still unremedied after the Marines had come and gone. There was not much publicity about that 1913 loan, not enough to disprove the detailed charges of the *Banco Nacional* that it was not awarded to the best bidder. Mr. Bryan was evidently assailed by doubts. He managed his personal finances well, but it is not certain that he was a competent judge of an intricate technical operation of this kind. While complete publicity would be as useless to the man in the street as the engineer's specifications on a suspension bridge, the knowledge that all the data were open to experts would give a certain confidence.

There was a great deal of dissatisfaction in Santo Domingo over the terms of the 1918 loan. Nothing was known of this in the United States. The claimants awarded less than $50 each were paid in cash, but $4,161,300 of the old Dominican floating debt was liquidated by turning over 20-year 5 percent bonds. Though the creditors were forced by Executive Order No. 193 of the Military Government to accept them, they could not be sold at par. There was no market for them in Santo Domingo, so the Military Government made a deal with "certain banking interests in the United States"[2] to take some at 87½ and the rest at 92. Thus the Dominican creditors got much less in cash than the face of their awards, and the foreign "banking interests" garnered a handsome profit.

The public did get possession of some details concerning the $2,500,000 issue of 1921 at 8 percent. These bonds also sold below par, so the actual yield to purchasers was much higher. All were taken up within a year and replaced by the 5½ percent bonds in 1922. Besides getting interest at a little over 9 percent, some of the 1921 purchasers collected a profit of about the same amount. Yet the general public has no way of knowing whether $2,500,000 could have been raised on better terms during the financial crisis of 1920-21, or whether it was advisable to take up the bonds in 1922 at a loss in order to avoid paying 2½ percent during their lifetime above the lower interest rate then current. "Representative" government is not very successful in these intricate financial matters. The interested financiers are a small informed group, the public a large and uninformed one; the governments have to consult the people who know, and who have the money.

In 1918, the Military Government was trying to get a floating debt funded for the smallest possible figure. Since there were Dominicans on the Claims Commission, the settlement was probably about as just as could be expected. This government of armed intruders was all-powerful. In fixing the interest rate on its bonds so that they could not be marketed at their face value, and then forcing the creditors to accept them, its zeal for economy led it into partial expropriation, though that ugly expression was not used. There can be no doubt that injustice was done. The American public never heard about it.

Perhaps the 1919 tariff law which the Americans made for Santo Domingo is an even better illustration of the main points indicated by these others. It was not a very wise measure, as the next three years showed. American trade was unduly favored. This was partially foreseen by the Military Government, which thought it would be a good thing. There is very little probability that a military group abroad will give an unfavorable account of its own activities. Most people honestly think fairly well of themselves. Military men, and the civilians they choose to help them in straightening out a foreign country, form a strongly patriotic group. The consular service gets the same type of person. Out of the moral excellence itself of this personnel arise some of the worst evils. The only gospel of uplift and progress these people know is Americanization. They may not be conscious imperialists at all, but their idea of improving Santo Domingo and the Dominicans is to follow the model of Ohio or New Jersey.

When the honest, efficient organizers try to Ohioize Santo Domingo or Haiti, they encounter resistance. The Dominicans or Haitians seem to be wrong-headed and unappreciative. Some Americans are always aware of the good intentions of many natives they meet. To the minds of this intellectual top layer of the intervention, the failure to "progress" is due to misunderstanding—on the part of the natives, of course. The way to get around the obstacle is to teach by example. It does not seem credible that anybody could see American plows, tractors, trucks and steam cranes at work without realizing that they must be generally adopted as soon as possible.

But the West Indies do not have the climate, people or social traditions of Ohio and New Jersey. The feverish zeal of these alien intruders for reaching material goals, abandoned before they are ever attained for others still farther off, is amusing but not always attractive to people whose idea of getting the most out of a short life is different. These Americans gobble up land at a terrifying rate, not because they have any real land-hunger whatever, but merely to get wealth quickly, and for the sheer nervous drive toward perennial activity.

Europeans as well as Latin-Americans have always been amazed at what Werner Sombart loved to call the "urbanization" of our American agriculture. What he meant was *commercialization*, but he was shading his terms in order to prove that the Jews were responsible for it. One explanation of the vogue of this German scholar's worst book (on the Jews and modern economic life) in Latin countries is that it seems to throw light on an otherwise inexplicable aspect of American civilization. It is much more probable that this curiously impersonal character of our economic organization is due to the use of machinery, arising from a historic plenitude of land and other natural resources, coupled with a relative scarcity and high cost of labor.

To Americanize West Indian agriculture would be—and has been in many places—a disaster for the natives. It leads to a few commercial crops, large holdings, a general landlessness of the native population, and economic vassalage. The perfect solution for the hardest Haitian problem was offered free by a group of French Catholic Brothers. They proposed to teach the Haitians how to farm their own plots to the best advantage, in the manner of southern Europe. But the Americans would have none of this. It was too fundamentally social, too slow, and not sufficiently mechanical. With the best of intentions, they imported American sugar, pineapple and cotton corporations. These tried to consolidate big holdings. Incidentally, they lost a lot of money for themselves, besides leading to the expenditure of Haitian public funds in experiments on crops which would evict native small holders if successful.

Potential friends of genuine reform are alienated, and thus harm rather than good is done, by general charges that our Government Departments are in a nefarious partnership with American big business. Again it is largely a case of a great deal of unconscious and much less conscious harm resulting from the left hand being a stranger to the activities of the right. Many facts are kept from the Government by Americans incorporated abroad. One of the reasons for such incorporations has been to get beyond the reach of taxation. If the earnings of stockholders were fully known, these people might have to pay out in personal income taxes what they save in corporation taxes. While the consulates promote business on the one hand, they are often singularly in the dark as to the financial details about corporations already planted.

Similarly, while the Bureau of Foreign and Domestic Commerce and other government agencies bring people together for business purposes, those benefited do not always explain their mutual affairs in detail to the agency concerned. Sooner or later, we may have to decide whether it is good democracy, statesmanship or business to maintain a great bureau, heavily financed by Congress out of national funds, which is solely devoted to helping Americans make money. Shortly after Secretary Hoover assumed office in 1921, he grouped these services to correspond as exactly as possible to the partitioning of big industry in the United States.

Information from Commercial Attachés, Trade Commissioners and Consuls all over the world, centers in this great Bureau of Foreign and Domestic Commerce. In other directions the wires run out to the seventeen district offices and thirty-five cooperative offices scattered over the United States. The correspondence is enormous. Reports are digested, information filed, and "trade opportunities" by the thousands published. Besides the regular publications, great numbers of special circulars are mimeographed. Not least in importance is the function of bringing people together—either with such officials as Trade Commissioners or with each other.

Some of this information is highly secret. The password is that one does *not* want enlightenment for any reason connected with the public interest, but purely for personal gain. There is no conspiracy of silence. The fact that this is a governmental machine for private moneymaking is due to the structure of our society, and its philosophy—in so far as it has one. Heads of groups in the Bureau are practical business men. This is not so much because the Government objects to a statesmanship which might consider long-time effects; it is rather to guarantee the single-minded efficiency of the men as immediate aids to dollar-getting.

There is a practical defense for the secrecy. Much information could never be collected except on the understanding that it is confidential. If one bank could find out from the Government what its rivals were planning, these would see that the leak did not occur next time. Financial information is the one kind hardest to get. Manufacturers and merchants are in somewhat the same position, however. To plan new business takes time, energy and money. Nobody likes to play cards with a mirror behind him.

From the standpoint of the general public, these technical services raise the most disturbing of the walls of secrecy. Back of them, we know that much is being forged which is vital to our future. Interventions are not being planned, but rather unconsciously prepared. Nobody is protecting our interests, or anybody's real interests, in the long run. The organization is as blind to anything excepting the immediate calls of digestion, as an anaconda in the process of swallowing.

The new buccaneers of finance and commerce have better manners than the old. They appeal to man's cupidity or threaten his standard of living where their predecessors used to tame him with a cutlass. No longer do governments hand out surreptitious letters of marque, or monarchs slyly take half the spoils. An age is dawning in which it is doubtful etiquette even to "say it with gunboats." The technique changes from one century to another, but the main objects are eternal. Buccaneers have never done a fraction of the damage inflicted by colonists and concessionnaires. The better their intentions, the worse it is for those they expropriate and displace.

Viewing imperialism as a melodrama does not get us anywhere. It is a process. The real "Yankee peril" in the Dominican Republic is the process of economically North-Americanizing the western hemisphere. Santo Domingo will probably never be heavily colonized from the United States—the climate will take care of that. But there is a danger that we may take the prosperity and leave her the posterity—a horde of laborers to make sugar for the coffee cups of the Temperate Zone.

REFERENCE NOTES BY CHAPTERS

CHAPTER I

1 (Page 3). John Hogan, an American envoy sent down in 1844, reported the population to be about half white. His report was finally printed in 1871: 41st Cong., 3rd Sess., H. of R. Ex. Doc. No. 42, 47 pp. John Bigelow and Horace Greeley attacked this conclusion in long series of articles in the *New York Evening Post* and the *New York Tribune*. Bigelow (*Retrospections of an Active Life,* Vol. I, p. 160) is authority for the statement that Sumner did not leave his seat in the Senate during the morning hour for six weeks—waiting to amend any resolution for Dominican recognition by adding "and Haiti."

2 (Page 4). Walsh, R. M., "My Mission to Saint Domingo," *Lippincott's Magazine*, March, 1871; Paxson, F. L., "A Tripartite Intervention in Haiti, 1851," *Univ. of Colorado Studies*, Vol. I, pp. 323-30.

3 (Page 4). McClellan's reports were printed in 1871: 41st Cong., 3rd Sess., H. of R. Ex. Doc. No. 43. David D. Porter, then a mere Lieutenant in the Navy, had been sent out in 1846. See his "Secret Missions to San Domingo," *North American Review*, Vol. CXXVIII, pp. 616-30.

Note on Sources

The indispensable original sources have been mentioned in the footnotes above, and need not be repeated. Judge Otto Schoenrich's general treaties, *Santo Domingo—A Country with a Future*, devotes the first four chapters to the period up to 1863. Dr. Mary Treudley's extremely good special study of American relations with Haiti and Santo Domingo to the close of our Civil War deserves to be much better known than it seems to be: "The United States and Santo Domingo—1789-1866," *Journal of Race Development*, Vol. VII, 1916-17, pp. 83-145; 220-274. For the general background of American diplomatic history, consult: John Bassett Moore, *Principles of American Diplomacy*; *Four Phases of American Development*; and *Digest of International Law*; J. B. Henderson, *American Diplomatic Questions*; R. G. Adams, *History of the Foreign Policy of the United States*. There is a vast literature on the Monroe Doctrine. To Moore's *Principles of American Diplomacy*, cited above, we may add two titles: W. R. Shephard, "The Monroe Doctrine Reconsidered," *Political Science Quarterly*, Vol. XXXIX, No. I, March, 1924; and D. S. Muzzey, *The United States of America*, Vol. I, pp. 321-8. J. H. Latané's *The United States in the Caribbean* is a standard treatise, but weak on Santo Domingo. Stephen Bonsal's *The American Mediterranean* is often cited, but should be avoided by the serious student. For the Spanish background, the one invaluable work is C. H. Haring, *Trade and Navigation Between Spain and the Indies in the Time of the Hapsburgs*. The references in this and the Schoenrich work cited above will furnish a starting point for anyone specially interested in this fascinating subject, which has been practically omitted here for want of space. The *Congressional Globe* (1837-74), predecessor of the *Congressional Record*, reports the debates. The biographical material on this period is endless. Miss Treudley's bibliography mentions enough to discourage the average reader.

CHAPTER II

1 (Page 7). A copy is preserved in the New York Public Library.
2 (Page 7). Howard's Hatch-San Domingo Report. Senate Report No. 234, 41st Cong. 2nd Sess., 1870. The interesting part is the minority report, signed by Carl Schurz and others, and the 265 pages of testimony. Grant's annexation project has usually been written up from the Report of the 1871 Commission: Sen. Ex. Doc. No. 9, 42nd Cong., 1st Sess., or even merely upon President Grant's letter transmitting it, which contained the famous thrust at Sumner as a "disappointed man." The actual testimony printed in the 1871 report has evidently not been read by most of the historians of the project. Damaging as some of it is to the position taken in the main body of the document, it gives a one-sided picture of the events, and must be checked up with the testimony given before the Senate Investigating Committee in the Hatch case.
3 (Page 8.) Special Report from the Select Committee on Loans to Foreign States, 1875, Appendix No. 33. This is in Vol. XI of the British Parliamentary Papers.
4 (Page 10). This is from the final one of the series, delivered in the Senate, March 27, 1871, entitled "Violations of International Law and Usurpations of War Powers," Sen. Ex. Doc. No. 34, 41st Cong. 2nd Sess. The "Naboth's Vineyard" speech of the preceding December is more often quoted, but it is much inferior. Sumner's final effort contained immoderate passages, but it was a logical and fairly complete summary of the case against the treaty, which it finally killed. He is one of the few contemporaries who appear to have carefully read the Hatch testimony.
5 (Page 11). The text of the two treaties was printed in the *New York Herald*, January 10, 1870.
6 (Page 12). E.g., *Foreign Relations of the United States*, 1870, pp. 6-8. There is a very temperate discussion of Sumner's part in the dispute in E. L. Pierce, *Memoir and Letters of Charles Sumner*, Vol. IV, pp. 429 ff.

Notes on Sources

Most of this material has been drawn from the works cited in footnotes, especially the Hatch investigation testimony and that taken by the Commission of 1871. Besides the prospectus of the American West India Company, there is a considerable collection of pamphlet and other material in the New York Public Library, all of which was examined. The file of the *New York Tribune* for two years from the middle of 1869, is a key to practically all the points raised against annexation at the time. E. P. Oberholtzer gives a good general account of the Santo Domingo annexation project in *A History of the United States since the Civil War*, Vol. II, pp. 225-44. Pierce's *Memoir and Letters of Charles Sumner*, Vol. IV, pp. 429 ff., throws a great deal of light on the circumstances surrounding Sumner's own speeches, and also the acts and utterances of other people. General W. L. Cazneau published an argument for annexation in Santo Domingo City in 1870, a copy of which is preserved in the Library of Congress ("To the American Press . . ."). The famous Patterson and Murguiondo case, over a guano island off the Dominican coast, has been omitted in the text because it did not seem to warrant the space it got in the press from 1860 to 1867. One of the final briefs, in pamphlet form in the New York Public Library, sum-

REFERENCE NOTES BY CHAPTERS 179

marized the charges of the ejected plaintiffs against the American Government for neglecting their interests, but it would seem that the State Department acted correctly. The Commissioners' Report of 1871 called forth quite an assortment of pamphlets and short books, notably two refutals printed by M. M. Zarzamendi in New York: *Brief Refutal of the Report of the St. Domingo Commissioners;* and *A Critical Review of the Report of the St. Domingo Commissioners.* The first was signed "Many Dominicans" and the second "Several Dominicans," though the latter at least was apparently the work of James Redpath, an American residing in Haiti who had already attacked the "roving band of Commissioners" in the *Boston Daily Advertiser.* Samuel G. Howe attempted to answer some of this literature in letters to periodicals, later (Boston, 1871) collected in a pamplet: *Letters on the proposed annexation of Santo Domingo.* President Grant's attitude is best summarized by himself in his annual message, printed in the 1870 volume of *Foreign Relations.* Samuel Hazard's old book *Santo Domingo* (1873) is interesting and vital, giving a good deal of detail about the country and the American colonists of that time. It was written from personal contact, as well as the reading of printed matter.

CHAPTER III

1 (Page 18). The details concerning the Hartmont loan will be found in the Select Committee Report on Loans to Foreign States, House of Commons, 1875 (cited in the previous chapter) and in Jacob H. Hollander's confidential report of 1905, entitled *The Debt of Santo Domingo.* This latter is a rare book, but two copies will be found in the library of the Pan-American Union at Washington. All the Westendorp and San Domingo Improvement Company agreements were printed in 1904 and used as exhibits in the Improvement Company arbitration. Copies were kindly lent the writer by Judge Otto Schoenrich and Professor John Bassett Moore, legal counsel for the two sides. On the Improvement Company's original right, see also *Gaceta Oficial* of Santo Domingo, No. 971, April 1, 1893, and *Foreign Relations of the United States,* 1906, Vol. I, p. 588. The troubles of the French *Banque Nationale* in 1895 are summarized in *Foreign Relations* for that year, Vol. I, pp. 235-43, 397-402. Its agreement will be found with the others in the briefs of the Improvement Company case, together with a vast literature in English and Spanish on the subject.

2 (Page 21). The above payment was one of the monthly installments, to continue at the same rate until definitive arrangements should be made by the commission of arbitration. *Foreign Relations* for the years following 1899 gives a fairly adequate general summary of the progress of these negotiations. The 1904 Improvement Company award is given in Exhibit "M" of the case, and also in the appendix to the Hollander report. It is somewhat abbreviated, but elaborately discussed, in Franco-Franco, *La Situation Internationale de la République Dominicaine* (Doctor's dissertation, University of Paris, 1923, 287 pp.), pp. 16-19.

3 (Page 22). Professor John Bassett Moore, *Argument of the United States,* January 31, 1903, pp. 95 ff.

4 (Page 23). This sketch is taken mainly from Juan J. Sanchez's little book, *La Caña en Santo Domingo,* published in Santo Domingo City in 1893.

5 (Page 24). These figures are from a sort of Dominican chronology prepared by the American Legation, printed in *Foreign Relations,* 1906, Vol. I, pp. 582 ff., and from the *First Annual Report of the Modus Vivendi Receivership,* p. 15 and Exhibit "N."

THE AMERICANS IN SANTO DOMINGO

Note on Sources

This chapter has been drawn largely from sixteen arguments and exhibits in the Improvement Company arbitration of 1903-4, thirteen for the Company and three for the Dominican Government. The other main sources used were: Jacob H. Hollander's 1905 confidential report entitled *The Debt of Santo Domingo;* the British Select Committee Report on the Hartmont loan mentioned in a footnote above; José Ramon Abad (Ed.), *La República Dominicana, Reseña General Geográfico-Estadística;* Senator Peligrin Castillo's *La Intervención Americana;* the annual volumes of *Foreign Relations,* and the *First Annual Report of the Modus Vivendi Receivership* (April 1, 1905 to March 31, 1906), which has a number of historical appendices. Various other books, pamphlets and files of newspapers were examined, but these sources are the main ones.

CHAPTER IV

1 (Page 26). *Foreign Relations,* 1905, pp. 360-61. Letter of March 28. See also Roosevelt's message transmitting the Protocol in the same volume, pp. 334-42. Also p. 5 of the *First Annual Receivership Report* (1905-6). Pages could be filled with references to the fictitiously spontaneous request.
2 (Page 26). *Op. cit.,* p. 298.
3 (Page 27). Roosevelt's action in taking the Canal Zone was not the only evidence of his views available in 1905. His threats to Germany two years earlier in the Venezuela dispute are well known. As early as 1898, while Assistant Secretary of the Navy, he had written: "I should myself like to shape American foreign policy with a purpose ultimately of driving off this continent every European power. I would begin with Spain, and in the end would take all other European nations, including England." Joseph B. Bishop, *Theodore Roosevelt and his Time,* Vol. I, p. 79.
4 (Page 28). *Foreign Relations,* 1905, p. 317.
5 (Page 28). *Op. Cit.,* p. 309.
6 (Page 29). The final draft, as submitted to the United States Senate, appears in *Foreign Relations,* 1905, pp. 342-343.
7 (Page 30). *Op. cit.,* p. 366. Text given in full.
8 (Page 32). Theodore Roosevelt, *An Autobiography,* pp. 507-511.
9 (Page 33). These facts and figures are taken from the Hollander Report, pp. 226-7, and from the *First Annual Modus Vivendi Report.*
10 (Page 36). The papers of the Bass trial are on pp. 617-20 of *Foreign Relations,* Part I, 1906. See also p. 616 of that volume and pp. 391 ff. of the one for 1905 for particulars of the sugar controversy.
11 (Page 38). Fabio Fiallo summarized the case, quoting extensively from the documents, in the *Listin Diario,* of Santo Domingo City, September 7 and 8, 1921. See the 1909 *Report of the Council of Foreign Bondholders,* London, pp. 307-324, and the 1925 volume, pp. 369-390.
12 (Page 38). Text of Convention in Treaty Series, No. 465, Washington, 1917. Also in Appendix C of Judge Schoenrich's *Santo Domingo—a Country with a Future,* in *Foreign Relations,* 1907, etc.
13 (Page 39). A. de la Rosa, "Les Finances de Saint-Domingue," *Revue de Droit International Public,* 1912, p. 106; P. Fauchille, *Traité de Droit International Public,* Vol. I, part I, p. 177 (1921); A. Viallate, *Economic Imperialism,* p. 66.

Note on Sources

Foreign Relations for 1905 and 1906, especially. After that, this source is less valuable. There are two Annual Reports of the Modus Vivendi Receivership (1906 and 1907) and a final summary. The *First Annual Report of the Official Receivership* (1907-1908) is indispensable. All of these annual reports, from the beginning to the present, are of the greatest importance, containing a vast amount of condensed, accurate information, especially on commerce. Constant use has been made of the *Gaceta Oficial* of the Dominican Republic, in which all laws and ordinances are published. The more important appear also in the *Listin Diario*, the one great Dominican daily newspaper of the period under discussion. This was used in Santo Domingo City, the file in the Pan-American Union at Washington dating only from 1909. From the angle of the international law and political relations, the book of Tulio Franco-Franco, *La Situation Internationale de la République Dominicaine à partir du 8 Février, 1907* (Paris, 1923, 287 pp.) is extremely useful.

CHAPTER V

1 (Page 41). The essential parts were printed in English as Exhibits "N" and "O" in the appendix of the *Second Annual Report of the Modus Vivendi Receivership*, and largely reprinted in Part I of *Foreign Relations*, 1907. Given in full in *Gaceta Oficial*, No. 1,770, 1907.

2 (Page 41). These words of Tejera's were wrongly attributed by Chester L. Jones (*Caribbean Interests of the United States*, pp. 115-16) to Velasquez. Roosevelt had used the example of Cuba in transmitting the 1905 Protocol to the Senate.

3 (Page 43). *Receptoria Aduanera, República de Santo Domingo, Reglamentos y Decisiones*, 1905-6, 220 pp. Also *Fourth Annual Report of Customs Receivership*, 1910-11, pp. 15-17 (on stoppage of frauds).

4 (Page 43). *Gaceta Oficial*, December 1, 1909, pp. 1-28. English text, *Dominican Customs Tariff*, Govt. Ptg. Office, Washington, 1910, 179 pp. This law was accompanied by one on customs and ports, *Gaceta Oficial*, December 4, 1909, pp. 1-8. See also *Gaceta Oficial*, August 6, 1910, for a municipal tax complication which arose; *Third Annual Report of Receivership* (1909-1910), pp. 9-14, and Fourth (1910-11), pp. 28-9.

5 (Page 45). "The Public Finance of Santo Domingo," *Political Science Quarterly*, December, 1918, pp. 461-481. A comprehensive report had been made to the Military Government under date of January 26, 1918.

6 (Page 47). The main facts about *comunero* or *peso* titles were summarized in the monthly *Consular Report*, November, 1909, No. 350, pp. 130-132. The system was also discussed in the 1871 Commissioners' Report and in the Hazard work cited in Chap. II above. The laws of 1907 and 1911 appear in Nos. 1,800 and 2,187 of the *Gaceta Oficial*. Only a perusal of Dominican newspaper files can give any real idea of the scope of the controversies between 1907 and 1919. The extremely important *Ley sobre Franquicias Agricolas*, under which most of the foreign sugar people operated, appears in the *Gaceta Oficial*, No. 2,207, July 8, 1911, pp. 1-3.

7 (Page 50). *Foreign Relations*, 1912, p. 366. Secretary Knox's speech of March 27 is in the same volume, pp. 389-390.

8 (Page 52). *Foreign Relations*, 1913, pp. 456-67, reprinted some of the correspondence about the loan. The whole history of it is obtainable only in the files of Dominican newspapers, the *Listin Diario* being the one chosen by the writer to turn through, page by page. Both the 1912 and 1913 volumes of *Foreign Relations* carry a great mass of material, under "Dominican Republic," on the Taft Commission and its attempts at a settlement. The Haitian boundary dispute, dealt with at length there, is omitted here, as any discussion of it would involve an exposition of the

situation in Haiti also, and would take too much space. For the celebrated case of the spurious Root speech, consult the *Congressional Record*, January 16, 1913, and *Foreign Relations*, 1913, pp. 4-6.

Note on Sources

The *Gaceta Oficial* is the mainstay. It is not one source, but a vast collection of them, running at that period into a huge bound volume per year, and now into two. As indicated in these notes, many of the laws were printed, some in both Spanish and English, under the auspices of the Receivership. The annual Receivership Reports, *Foreign Relations*, and newspaper files furnished most of remainder of the material for this chapter. It should be glanced through in the original by the serious student, if for no other reason, merely to remind him what an enormous mass of facts it has been necessary to omit here, picking only what seemed most important and representative. The work of Franco-Franco, cited in the preceding chapter, also presents many documents, translated from Spanish into French. I think I have read all the prospectuses and other pamphlet material on the subject in the library of the Pan-American Union at Washington. The two mentioned in the text are worth reading entire, for those in reach of them and having the time. As indicated by the volume of the *Reader's Guide to Periodical Literature*, there were a great many magazine articles on Santo Domingo, some of them pertinent; but on the whole I have found them patched together from secondary sources and unreliable. Max Henriquez Ureña's *Los Estados Unidos y la Republica Dominicana*, Chap. IV (Habana, 1919), deals briefly with this period, and is better for the later ones. It is perhaps the best, and the most fully documented, single volume on the antecedents of the marine occupation of 1916.

CHAPTER VI

1 (Page 54). The sketch of Sullivan's early career was taken from the *Santo Domingo Investigation—Copy of the Report, Findings and Opinions of James D. Phelan*, Washington, 1916, 32 pp., and the files of the *New York Times* and the *New York Tribune*. The Report was based on the 3,491 pp. of testimony and 394 exhibits of the official investigation, in which ninety-three witnesses were examined.

2 (Page 57). *Foreign Relations*, 1913, pp. 427-436. This covers the instructions and also the correspondence covering Minister Sullivan's negotiations for a truce.

3 (Page 57). *Foreign Relations*, 1913, pp. 439-440, December 2 and 5. The "Wilson declaration" referred to is evidently the State Department circular-telegram of March 12, 1913, printed on p. 7 of the same volume. Every student of the Wilsonian Latin-American policy should make himself thoroughly familiar with this document. Its language does not justify Sullivan's extreme statement.

4 (Page 59). The document in question appears in *Foreign Relations*, 1914, pp. 247-8.

5 (Page 61). *Foreign Relations*, 1914, p. 256.

6 (Page 63). *Foreign Relations*, 1915, pp. 311-13. Spanish version, copied from the archives of the Dominican Legation, Henriquez Ureña, *Los Estados Unidos y la Republica Dominicana*, p. 69. This was translated by Franco-Franco into French, in his book cited in the last chapter.

REFERENCE NOTES BY CHAPTERS 183

Note on Sources

Add to the *Gaceta Oficial*, the Annual Receivership Reports, *Foreign Relations* and the newspaper files, the work of Max Henriquez Ureña, *Los Estados Unidos y la Republica Dominicana*. This book grows fuller and more important as we approach the 1916 American intervention. *El Tiempo* and *La Bandera Libre* should be added to the *Listin Diario* as newspapers to be consulted. Franco-Franco, as cited in the preceding chapter, is fullest on questions of constitutional and international law. James D. Phelan's *Santo-Domingo Investigation—Copy of the Report, Findings and Opinions*, summarized the Sullivan case, which occupied much space in the New York and Washington daily papers at the beginning of 1915. The Receivership prepared an important *Summary of Commerce, Dominican Republic*, published by the Bureau of Insular Affairs in March, 1914.

CHAPTER VII

1 (Page 69). *Foreign Relations*, 1915, pp. 321-25.
2 (Page 69). No. 14 covers pp. 333-337 of *Foreign Relations*, 1915.
3 (Page 71). The resignation was printed as a circular and copied by the daily papers of May 7. The text is in Henriquez Ureña, *op. cit.*, pp. 85-86. It was addressed to the people, not the Congress, and thus failed to comply with the terms of the Constitution.
4 (Page 72). *Hearings*, Vol. II, p. 1,097.
5 (Page 73). The text of the ultimatum was printed in *El Tiempo* and the *Listin Diario*. It appears in Henriquez Ureña, *op. cit.*, pp. 89-90. See *Foreign Relations*, 1916, pp. 226 ff., for the American correspondence about it.
6 (Page 73). Published in the daily papers, May 15. See *Foreign Relations*, 1916, pp. 229 ff., for somewhat abridged and softened record of this correspondence.
7 (Page 74). Printed in full in Henriquez Ureña, p. 95.
8 (Page 75). Letter printed in Henriquez Ureña, p. 103. The protest of all the Ministers, the notice of Receiver Baxter, and the final letter of Finance Minister Jimenez, stating that he had no further means of forcing the United States to respect the 1907 Convention, follow in the next five pages.
9 (Page 78). This is perfectly clear in the correspondence, signed by President Wilson, Secretary Lansing, Minister Russell, Clerk Brewer, and Mr. Stabler (Chief of the Division of Latin-American Affairs in the State Department), as printed in the 1916 volume of *Foreign Relations*, pp. 240 ff. Stabler wrote as follows: "The withholding of the funds by the United States Government . . . has brought an economic crisis in the country which is daily growing worse and for which this Government would not wish to be placed in a position that it would be held responsible."
10 (Page 82). Testimony from *Hearings*, Vol. II, pp. 1,094-95.
11 (Page 84). The report in question is quoted at length in *Hearings*, Vol. I, pp. 94 ff.

Note on Sources

Much of this material is from the files of the newspapers mentioned in the previous chapter. The 1916 volume of *Foreign Relations*, the first under Mr. Tyler Dennett's editorship, is much better than its immediate predecessors, going back to the best traditions of earlier years. It needs to be checked with Henriquez Ureña's *Los Estados Unidos y La República Dominicana*, which is fuller on some matters. Henriquez Ureña was the President's Secretary, and had access to the documents in Spanish. The section in Franco-Franco's book (previously cited) which deals with this period is largely based on the above work. Some readers will prefer it because it is in French. Two other sources should be mentioned, as giving some material not in those above: Emilio Roig de Leuchsenring, *La Ocupación de la República Dominicana por los Estados Unidos y el Derecho de las pequeñas Nacionalidades de America;* and Tulio M. Cestero, *Los Estados Unidos y la República Dominicana.* The first has been printed in booklet form. It was an address delivered by an eminent Cuban jurist before the Cuban International Law Society in 1919. Cestero's two articles under the above title appeared in *La Reforma Social,* Tomo IX (1916-17), No. 1, pp. 74-103, and No. 2, pp. 66-112. The *Hearings* referred to in the footnotes are those of the Senate Investigating Committee (2 vols., 67th Cong., 1st & 2nd Sess., pursuant to Senate Resolution No. 112). The *Gaceta Oficial* of Santo Domingo is hardly obtainable complete for the period when the Americans were withholding Dominican public funds. When it appeared, it was printed on a wretched quality of paper which is already crumbling as though it had been heated. Most of the important governmental acts appeared in the *Listin Diario,* a file of which is available in the Columbus Memorial Library, Pan-American Union, Washington, D. C. Many errors in the contemporary accounts could be corrected when the American Government finally published the correspondence of 1916, ten years later, in *Foreign Relations.*

CHAPTER VIII

1 (Page 87). *Gaceta Oficial,* December 27, 1916.
2 (Page 87). *Op. Cit.,* January 6, 1917.
3 (Page 88). Tenth Fiscal Period, Appendix A, Schedule No. 5.
4 (Page 88). Lt. Commander A. H. Mayo, *Report of the Department of State of Finance and Commerce* . . ., issued 1920 (Campaign year in the United States!), p. 6. *Santo Domingo, its Past and Present Condition,* Santo Domingo City, 1920, p. 7.
5 (Page 90). *Gaceta Oficial,* December 9, 1916. The order was dated December 4.
6 (Page 90). Ex. Ord. No. 20 appeared in the *Gaceta Oficial,* January 10, 1917; No. 21, removing Sr. Morillo from the post at Havana, January 17.
7 (Page 90). No. 44, *Gaceta Oficial,* March 24, 1917.
8 (Page 91). *Hearings,* Vol. I, pp. 94-95. Robison quotes Knapp at length, and then proceeds to lay down the "doctrine." Knapp was the first Military Governor, Robison the last.
9 (Page 92). *Foreign Relations,* 1916, pp. 244-245. Secretary Lansing gave a synopsis of its points in a telegram to Minister Russell, *op. cit.,* p. 248. The works of Franco-Franco and Roig de Leuchsenring, already mentioned, are good examples of the position commonly taken in Latin America. Henríquez Ureña's book (largely documents) *Los Estados Unidos y la República Dominicana* . . . was the one which finally crystallized the Dominçan argument on all the main points and important details.
10 (Page 93). "The Armed Occupation of Santo Domingo," under "Editorial Comments" in the *American Journal of International Law,* April, 1917, Vol. II, pp. 394-99. Franco-Franco (*op. cit.,* pp. 116-21) points out that this was accepted by various European authorities as the standard American apology for the occupation. This must have been a surprise to the author, as the brief and casual nature of the "comment" does not suggest that it was intended for any such dissection.

REFERENCE NOTES BY CHAPTERS

11 (Page 96). Emilio Roig de Leuchsenring, *La Ocupación de la República Dominicana* . . . (1919), pp. 45 ff.

Note on Sources

The *Gaceta Oficial*, the newspaper files already mentioned, the two volumes of *Senate Committee Hearings* (1921-2, 67th Cong., 1st & 2nd Sess., Sen. Res. No. 112) and *Foreign Relations* for 1916 and 1917 contain the bulk of the materials. The last of these volumes was used in galley proof. A volume of *Documentos Historicos* . . ., edited by Antonio Hoepelman and Juan A. Senior, appeared in Santo Domingo City in 1922. It duplicates much of the contents of the *Hearings*, but also gives other documents. A copy of the Roig de Leuchsenring pamphlet will be found in the New York Public Library. *La Reforma Social* of Havana and New York carried a number of articles which help to convey the Latin-American point of view, and also throw some fresh light on the facts. Two by Cestero are cited above in the reference notes. The general works of Franco-Franco and Henriquez Ureña, previously cited, continue to be indispensable.

CHAPTER IX

1 (Page 99). *Report of Department of State of Finance and Commerce*, 1916-1919, p. 16.

2 (Page 100). *Report of Department of State of Finance and Commerce*, 1916-19, pp. 55-59.

3 (Page 100). *Hearings*, Vol. I, pp. 90-104, Section on Finances, pp. 97-99.

4 (Page 101). *Annual Report on Commerce and Industries*, 1924, p. 2.

5 (Page 102). From a *ms.* report in the Department of Commerce dated January 20, 1925. There is a complete report written by a Dominican engineer, M. A. Cocco, and published by the Pan-American Union, *La Reconstruction de un Pueblo*. He puts the cost higher than Minister Russell.

6 (Page 103). Dated January 26, 1918. See the "Public Finance of Santo Domingo," *Political Science Quarterly*, December, 1918, pp. 461-81.

7 (Page 103). Internal Revenue Law, *Gaceta Oficial*, September 4, 1918, pp. 50-83. Ex. Ord. No. 197; Tariff Law, Ex. Ord. No. 332, *Gaceta Oficial*, October 1, 1919, No. 3,051. For a thoroughly prejudiced summary see Mayo's *Report of the Department of State of Finances and Commerce*, 1916-1919, pp. 32-33. Real Property Tax, Ex. Ord. No. 282, *Gaceta Oficial*, May 7, 1919, No. 3,009-B, pp. 3-38.

8 (Page 103). Spanish text in *Gaceta Oficial*, July 31, 1920; English, September 1, 1920.

9 (Page 104). 1920 *Annual Receipt Report*, p. 3. See also 1919 Report, p. 3 and 1921 Report, p. 1.

10 (Page 105). Dated May 19, 1920. *Gaceta Oficial*, May 29, 1920, No. 3,120.

Note on Sources

The *Gaceta Oficial*, the annual Customs Receivership Reports and the newspaper files are the fundamental checks on the facts. There are a few sets of collected Executive Orders, which save time where available, though all the Orders had appeared in the *Gaceta*. Mayo's *Report of Department of State of Commerce and Finance for the Period of 1916 to 1919 inclusive, and Estimates for 1920* is the leading defense of Marine finance.

Closely related to it is the Military Government's 1920 pamphlet: *Santo Domingo, its Past and Present Condition.* There is an interesting Navy Department Memorandum, dated August 5, 1921, in the *Hearings* of the Senate Committee of Enquiry, 1921-22, Vol. I, pp. 90-104. In Vol. II of the *Hearings,* pp. 1,279-1,341, appears a reprint of Professor Carl Kelsey's: *The American Intervention in Haiti and the Dominican Republic* (also in the *Arnals of American Academy of Political and Social Science* for 1922). Interesting papers by Judge Schoenrich and Colonel Thorpe are printed in *Mexico and the Caribbean,* edited by G. H. Blakeslee and published by Stechert in New York (1920). Most of the ammunition for the attacks made by Dominicans and others at the time upon the Military Government's financial methods were drawn, directly or indirectly, from Francisco J. Peynado's *Informe Sobre La Situacion Economica y Financiera de la República Dominicana* . . . (Santo Domingo, 1922, printed separately, and also in the Hoepelman y Senior *Documentos Historicos* . . .)

CHAPTER X

1 (Page 108). Judge Otto Schoenrich, in *Mexico and the Caribbean,* p. 212 (Blakeslee, Editor). This paper at the 1920 Clark University Conference was followed by that of Colonel Thorpe, mentioned below.

2 (Page 109). *Hearings,* Vol. II, pp. 1,130 ff.

3 (Page 110). *Hearings,* Vol. II, pp. 1,117 ff.

4 (Page 111). There are a great many cases mentioned in the *Hearings,* in Judge Schoenrich's paper, mentioned above, and in the famous letter of Archbishop Nouel to Minister Russell, December 29, 1920, published in the Hoepelman and Senior, *Documentos Historicos,* pp. 11-13. A book could be filled with them from the files of the *Listin Diario* alone.

5 (Page 117). *Gaceto Oficial,* December 8, 1920, No. 3,175.

Note on Sources

Newspaper files, the *Gaceta Oficial,* the *Hearings* of the Senate Committee, the volume edited by Blakeslee on *Mexico and the Caribbean,* and the collection of *Documentos Historicos by* Hoepelman and Senior are important general sources. The Fabio Fiallo trial material was taken from a typewritten copy of the official American transcript, furnished to the accused, who was visited by the author at his home in La Vega. He also lent the writer a huge volume of newspaper clippings about the affair, from all over the world. Space limitations have made it necessary to crowd out a mass of most interesting material on this case, and to omit entirely the trials of the other author, Americo Lugo, and the publisher.

CHAPTER XI

1 (Page 120). *Listin Diario,* September 7 and 8, 1921.

2 (Page 120). *Hearings,* Vol. II p. 953.

3 (Page 121). *Informe Sobre la Situacion Economica y Financiera de la República Dominicana, y el Modo de Solucionar sus Problemas.*

4 (Page 121). The State Department had released to the press a long communication on Santo Domingo, dated December 24, 1920. The American Government proposed to appoint a "technical advisor" to work with a "Commission of representative Dominican citizens" in amending the Dominican constitution and revising the laws. If this new body of law were approved by a Constitutional Convention and a National Congress,

REFERENCE NOTES BY CHAPTERS 187

Santo Domingo would then assume as much independence as the new Constitution allowed. The actual terms appeared in the *Gaceta Oficial* for July 9 and October 5, 1921.

5 (Page 123). Peynado (pp. 23-4) quotes the Robison report at length. It had been addressed to the Chamber of Commerce, Industry and Agriculture in the Dominican Capital, December 3, 1921.

6 (Page 124). Printed in 1925 *Report of Customs Receivership*, pp. 98-106.

7 (Page 124). The oath was rather to the Commission, under the Evacuation Agreement, than to the Republic, which had no effective constitution. See *Gaceta Oficial*, October 21-25, 1922.

8 (Page 124). Internal revenue figures in *Memoria Correspondiente al Año 1924*, by Dr. J. D. Alfonseca (Minister of Commerce and Finance). For customs collections see 1924 *Receivership Report*, p. 1.

9 (Page 125). *Gaceta Oficial*, June 21, 1924, No. 3,550, English translation by W. C. Wells of the Pan American Union Staff, Washington, 1925 (Law and Treaty Series, No. 1).

10 (Page 126). At the end of 1924, the face value of outstanding bonds was $15,140,950, but the net sum due was reduced by assets in the sinking fund to $13,534,276.14. The 1924 loan of $2,500,000, placed with Lee, Higginson & Co. at 5½ percent, was considered the tenth part of the new consolidated one. (*Receivership Report*, 1924, pp. 3-7).

11 (Page 126). There were political complications also. The new convention was ratified by doubtfully constitutional methods in Santo Domingo, (May, 1925); but the same reservations as to the meaning of its terms were adopted as in the case of the 1907 documents. The 1925 Convention is No. 726, Treaty Series, Government Printing Office, 1925. For Dominican reservations, see *Gaceta Oficial*, May 27, 1925.

12 (Page 126). 1925 *Receivership Report*, pp. 4-6, summarizes loan service activities.

13 (Page 126). *Ley No. 190, Con Sus Modificaciones y Reglementos para el Corbro del Impuesto en Ella Establecido*, Edicion oficial, Santo Domingo, 1926. The chief modifications are in Laws 268, 278 and 346. These and various regulations are all included in the volume.

14 (Page 127). Schedule 5, Appendix C, 1925 *Receivership Report*.

15 (Page 128). That this group of laws, the tariff and the land tax were all bound up together was clearly recognized by the Minister of Finance and Commerce in his 1925 Report. *Gaceta Oficial*, March 20, 1926, No. 3,735.

Note on Sources

Besides those given in the last chapter, the work of Felix E. Mejia, *Al Rededor y en Contra del Plan Hughes-Peynado*, is well-worth reading. Considerable use of Consular Reports has been made in preparing this chapter—both the annual ones and the great mass of *mss.* from 1922 to the end of 1925 (in the Department of Commerce at Washington). A detailed *Memoria* of the Dominican Government Department of Finance is published annually. The similar one for *Fomento y Comunicaciones* (Public Works, Transportation, etc.) is larger than the present book each year. The newspaper material has been read as it appeared during 1925-26. Files get more and more unmanageable with the increasing size and number of papers; the Pan-American Union ceased to bind them years ago.

CHAPTER XII

1 (Page 130). *Moody's Manual of Railroads and Corporation Securities, Industrial Section* (Annual).

2 (Page 136). Lopez, Jose R., *La Industria Azucarera*, 1916. Lopez was

the Director General of Statistics. The figures for 1923 are from the *Receivership Report*, p. 11. Those for 1924-26 were taken from consular reports filed in the Bureau of Foreign and Domestic Commerce. The Las Pajas mill had even a more startling growth, but it was new and the figures might be misleading.

3 (Page 140). *Gaceta Oficial*, September 1, 1920 (English version) Ex. Ord. No. 511.

Note on Sources

This chapter is based largely on personal observations and interviews in Santo Domingo. In a supplementary way, many documents have been used. These include statements furnished by the Dominican Government Departments of Finance and Public Works; the annual reports (*Memoria*) of the Secretaries of State heading those Departments, and a mass of consular report, largely in *ms*. As usual, the Receivership Reports have been used. The *Segunda Edición* (1925) of the *Directorio Industrial y Comercial*, published by Luis P. Peynado in Santo Domingo City, is particularly valuable because of the advertisements it carries, which give a good idea of the foreign trading concerns, banks, etc. The *Gaceta Oficial* is the one check on governmental acts, economic as well as more strictly political. Willett & Gray's *Weekly Statistical Trade Journal* gives the current world news about sugar. Their statistical service is indispensable for detailed technical work. This is expensive and, like the sugar trade journals, is best consulted in the offices of companies or men in the trade. Moody's *Manual of Railroads and Corporation Securities, Industrial Section*, years since 1916, has been checked with the *New York Directory of Directors* and similar manuals for the interlocking or overlapping of directors, besides other information. Sugar firms often issue very interesting little pamphlets. For example, Farr & Co. prepared a helpful *Manual of Sugar Companies* in 1925, with price tables drawn from U. S. Tariff Commission data.

CHAPTER XIII

1 (Page 149). 1925 Receivership Report, schedule 5, Appendix C.

2 (Page 151). Advertisement in Washington *Post*, January 24, 1926, cited in an article by Jacinto Lopez in *La Reforma Social* for the following March: "La Tragedia de las Riquezas Dominicanas."

3 (Page 152). E.g., an open letter to the Secretary of the Interior, published March 18, 1926, in *El Esfuerzo*, a Barahona newspaper, under the title: "Devastacion de Nuestros Bosques."

4 (Page 155). Figures from M. A. Cocco, *La Reconstruccion de un Pueblo* p. 14, and 1925 Receivership Report, Appendix C., Schedule No. 1.

5 (Page 157). The main facts about this concession were given in a *ms*. Consular Report of June 30, 1925.

6 (Page 157). *Report of the Economic, Financial and Commercial Conditions in Dominican Republic and Republic of Haiti*, September, 1925, H. M. Stationery Office, London. The details of the labor troubles were picked up by interviews with British citizens in Santo Domingo. One of the main complaints was that the Italians neither insured their men nor sent them home when injured, according to the American practice. Housing conditions are worse, on the whole, on the Italian estates, though the Haitian settlements are pretty bad even at la Romana and Barahona. As Shakespeare remarked, there is "small choice twixt rotten apples."

7 (Page 158). There were two editorials on the Haitian menace in the *Listin Diario*, March 4 and 5, 1924. The American Minister (then W. W.

Russell) wrote the Secretary of State a long letter of comment upon them, March 8, a copy of which the writer happened to find and read.

Note on Sources

This chapter is based on notes taken on the ground in the winter and spring of 1926, and on various manuscript material in the Government files at Washington, including detailed Consular Reports. As usual, this has been checked and supplemented by the use of the Receivership Reports, the *Gaceta Oficial* and Dominican newspapers. The second, 1925, edition of the *Directorio Industrial y Comercial*, published by Luis P. Peynado in Santo Domingo City, is invaluable. The *Memoria* of Dr. J. D. Alfonseca, Minister of Finance and Commerce, was checked with figures from the 1925 copy, which was still in *ms.* when this chapter was prepared. The summary of finances for 1925 appeared in the *Gaceta Oficial* for March 20, 1926. M. A. Cocco's *La Reconstruccion de un Pueblo*, previously cited, contains an interesting study of the effects of the new roads in lowering the prices of country produce at the markets. It did not seem practicable to summarize this within the present space limitations. *The British Consular Report of the Economic, Financial and Commercial Conditions in the Dominican Republic and Republic of Haiti* (H. M. Stationery Office, London, September, 1925) is well worth perusing.

CHAPTER XIV

1 (Page 164). *Gaceta Oficial*, March 20, 1926, No. 3,735, p. 11.

2 (Page 170). *Santo Domingo, Its Past and Its Present Condition*, p. 11. Executive Orders Nos. 193 and 272, dealing with the 1918 bond issue, were printed in Mayo's *Report of the Department of Finance and Commerce*, pp. 61-2; 76-84.